Does she...or doesn't she?

If I've only one life . . . let me live it as a blonde!

THE BLONDE

THE BLONDE

A CELEBRATION OF THE GOLDEN ERA FROM HARLOW TO MONROE

Barnaby Conrad III

CHRONICLE BOOKS

SAN FRANCISCO

Page 128 constitutes a continuation of the copyright page.

Library of Congress Cataloging-in-Publication Data:

Conrad, Barnaby, 1952–

    The blonde : a celebration of the golden era from Harlow to

  Monroe / Barnaby Conrad III.

    p.   cm.

      Includes bibliographical references and index.

      ISBN 0-8118-2591-4

      1. Blondes. 2. Actresses. 3. Feminine beauty (Aesthetics)

  I.   Title.

GT6737.C65 1999

391.6' 082—dc21   99-22312

                                                CIP

  Printed in Hong Kong.

Book and cover design: Tom Morgan, Blue Design

Distributed in Canada by Raincoast Books

8680 Cambie Street

Vancouver, British Columbia V6P 6M9

10 9 8 7 6 5 4 3 2 1

Chronicle Books

85 Second Street

San Francisco, California 94105

www.chroniclebooks.com

For my sisters Tani and Kendall, with love

ACKNOWLEDGMENTS:

I wish to thank Mark Miller and Andrew Nelson for their suggestions and editing skills; Fiona Brandon and Bill Broyles for their persistent research on text and photographs; Tom Morgan for his book design; my agent, Fred Hill, for making the deal; Jay Schaefer and Steve Mockus for their guidance in the editing stage; Adrienne Gordon, Sarah Woodberry, and Alex Parent for their blonde inspiration and friendship; Rick Bolen for his speedy camera work; and Robert Johnson for sharing his photography collection. Finally, I'd like to express my gratitude to all the blondes, natural or otherwise, who have made life so interesting for this restless bachelor.

—BCIII

Opposite: Three blondes on water skis, circa 1940.

Page 2: Blondes exemplified a sporty sensuousness in America during the 1960s.

Page 4: Wynne Gibson was one of the most popular blondes in early Hollywood, the star of such films as Children of Pleasure *(1930) and* Flirting with Fate *(1938); she is depicted here with a 1933 license plate.*

Page 5: Blondes fought their own battles. This postcard from the 1940s is a far cry from the demure blonde ice princess.

Pages 8–9: In The Postman Always Rings Twice *(MGM, 1946), Lana Turner played a dangerous blonde who drives her lover, James Garfield, to kill her husband, Cecil Kellaway.*

Page 10: Roy Lichtenstein, Frightened Girl, *1964. Oil on canvas. 48 x 48 inches. (©Estate of Roy Lichtenstein. Photo: Robert McKeever)*

Page 11: Marilyn Monroe struggled to be taken seriously. "I wanted to be an artist, not an erotic freak," she said.

CONTENTS

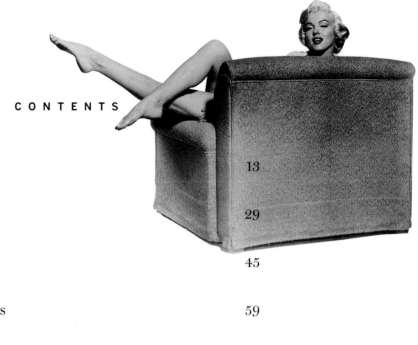

Introduction   13

The Dye Is Cast   29

Top Billing   45

Literature and Politics   59

The Golden Blonde   77

Va-va-voom   95

Epilogue: Gallery of Postmodern Blondes   117

Bibliography   127

Picture Credits   128

Index   129

INTRODUCTION

"It was a blonde. A blonde to make a bishop kick a hole in a stained-glass window."
—RAYMOND CHANDLER, *Farewell My Lovely*

More than a hair color, being blonde in the twentieth century embodied a feminine mystique, a philosophical aura, and a fashion statement that set the adventurous woman apart. Blondeness by birth or by choice offered possibilities, dreams, and expectations. *Is it true blondes have more fun?*

The word *blonde* conjures up a world of golden-tressed fairytale princesses, steamy Hollywood stars, aloof Park Avenue heiresses, dreamy *Playboy* centerfolds, sensible farm girls from Kansas, haughty German baronesses, doll-like ballerinas, tough-talking gangsters' molls, scheming chorus girls, saintly madonnas, and fresh-faced Olympic swimmers smiling in glory. But how much difference does hair color make in the lives of women and the men who admire them? Would dark tresses have changed the destiny of Mae West, Clare Booth Luce, Marilyn Monroe, and anthropologist Jane Van Lawick-Goodall? What about Evita Peron, Grace Kelly, and Diana Spencer?

The Golden Era of the Blonde embraces the decades between World War I and the Vietnam War, from the rise of Jean Harlow to

Above: In California in the 1930s sunny blondes were as plentiful as the grapes they sold.

Opposite: Born Harlean Carpenter, Jean Harlow became the first great Hollywood blonde. A natural blonde as a child, she pushed her hair color to a silvery platinum that inspired legions of women to do the same.

Right: This Italian Lines advertisement featuring sun-bleached blondes appeared in Fortune *magazine in March 1939.*

Opposite: Blondes have more fun on a roller coaster at the Southend fair, Essex, England, 1938.

So bright the sun

It gleams from bronzed shoulders, shimmers on the open-air pools and decks. Even in early Spring . . . even before you reach the blue, luminous Mediterranean . . . every day is "beach" day on a Lido liner!

Pleasant shipmates share the sunny outdoor play, the worldly entertainment. Throughout your voyage you live splendidly . . . dine sumptuously . . . enjoy Lido's incomparable stewardship . . . when you cross to Europe on the mild Southern Route.

Choose the Rex or gyro-stabilized Conte di Savoia for speed . . . or, for a more leisurely crossing, select the Roma, Saturnia or Vulcania, or Italian Line. Consult your TRAVEL AGENT or Italian Line, 624 Fifth Ave., New York. Offices in Philadelphia, Boston, Cleveland, Chicago, Los Angeles, San Francisco, New Orleans, Montreal, Toronto.

Italian Line

the demise of Marilyn Monroe. There were blondes before and blondes after, yet in this half century the message seemed to be that, while black, brown, auburn, and red hair were each beautiful in their way, blonde was the most noticed and the most desired hair color. It meant something special—sometimes good, sometimes naughty— to be blonde.

In literature, quintessential high society was blonde: Jordan Baker in Fitzgerald's *The Great Gatsby* had hair that was a variety of "autumn leaf yellow." But there were blondes in all stations in life. Take

the opening line to "The Wild Party," Joseph Moncure March's scandalous 1932 poem: "Queenie was a blonde and her age stood still,/ And she danced twice a day in vaudeville." Now think of the phrase, "He ran off with a blonde chorus girl." Would "a *brunette* chorus girl" deliver the same impact?

Pulp literature and a few classic novels made much of the blonde, but it was the dramatic shadows and silver-nitrate highlights of the early movies that imprinted her deeply into the American psyche. The heyday of the Hollywood Blonde began in the 1930s when Jean Harlow became the premier platinum goddess of Tinseltown. The wisecracking Harlow beguiled audiences with what film maven Leslie Halliwell called "a likable impudence" that was electrifying to men and inspiring to women. Her on-screen glamour set a standard for females not only in Hollywood but around the world. From then on,

Above: This blonde is of indeterminate age but unquestionably provocative, a pre-Nabokovian Lolita. The 1930s saw an explosion of pulp magazines, including Pep, *which offered "spicy" and "snappy" stories for the male market—tame by today's standards.*

Left: The blonde ranged from "the kid" to "the temptress"—often in the same woman, as portrayed in this 1940 Collier's *magazine cover.*

*Left: The natural blonde
was perceived as
upperclass, aristocratic;
the dyed blonde was
thought to be "fast" until
hair coloring became ac-
ceptable after World War
II. This illustration is
from* American *magazine
circa 1938.*

blondes were perceived differently and watched more closely. With the new hair dyes, anyone could become more like Harlow simply by becoming a blonde.

Blondes tell us something about the zeitgeist of different eras. Mae West, the Great Blonde Philosopher-Dame who emerged during the Flapper Era, was what Halliwell described as the "American leading lady of the Thirties, the archetypal sex symbol, splendidly vulgar, mocking, overdressed and endearing." West, who wrote most of her stage plays and scripts, exuded a confident, controlling blondeness, the sign of a woman who knew she could get what she wanted when

Right: Mae West as she appeared in her hit play Diamond Lil *in 1934. In transforming herself into a wisecracking vaudevillian diva, Mae West created a signature style that she employed, with few changes, throughout her life.*

Opposite: A Prussian by birth, Marlene Dietrich brought an exotic glamour to Hollywood in the 1930s.

BLONDES LEAD WONDERFUL LIVES

BY ELEANOR POLLOCK, *GOOD HOUSEKEEPING*, FEBRUARY 1955

Not being a blonde myself, I am going to be accused of sour grapes. But even the taste of that bitter berry doesn't deter me from saying what I think. And what I think is that blondes are unfair. Blondes lead wonderful lives—and they don't do a thing to deserve it. Their yellow hair seems sufficient reason for their being. And unlike the rest of us, who, like Saturday's children, work for what we get, all blondes have to do is exist. Everything else is done for them. By men, what's more. Sometimes I think every woman should be a blonde at least once!

Why the sight of a blonde should start otherwise sensible men drooling like idiots is something I have never understood. Or why a man should decide that because a girl is blonde she can't, and what is more doesn't need to, tell the time of day, open a door, or boil water, all things any woman with any color hair is supposed to be born knowing, is beyond me. But we might as well face the fact that blondes, natural or self-induced, seem automatically to bring out all the "best" instincts latent in a human male.

And believe me, the girls with the yellow hair know it. They don't miss a trick. And why should they? They can knock on any door and it swings back for them. Given a choice of a blonde or a brunette, nine times out of ten any man will take vanilla. Not only for a date but a job, too. Those cartoons about blonde secretaries aren't just the ditherings of some frustrated artist. They have their basis in sound, hard facts. I wager here and now that, given two girls, a blonde and a brunette of equal ability, age, and poise, the average man looking for a girl Friday will pick the blonde. Maybe subconsciously, but the fix is in.

Long ago I learned not to try to compete with blondes on even ground. How many parties have you gone to and suddenly discovered all the men buzzing around a little blonde queen bee who was making time as well as honey? If it hasn't happened to you, sister, you haven't lived.

Opposite: Marilyn Meseke was Miss America in 1938—and a blonde.

20

Left: Ginger Rogers and Fred Astaire cutting the rug in Swing Time *(RKO Pictures, 1936).*

Opposite: Blondes drew attention to themselves around the world. Here Kim Novak—one of Alfred Hitchcock's favorite actresses—parts a mob of photographers at the Cannes Film Festival in 1956.

Right: Clark Gable and Carole Lombard circa 1935. The classic screen called for a strong dark-haired male lead and a blonde beauty.

Director and leading man Orson Welles convinced auburn Rita Hayworth to dye her hair blonde in 1948 for Lady from Shanghai *(Columbia Pictures, 1948). Rita later went back to her original color.*

she wanted it. Her platinum mane was an advertisement and a lure, but also a marcelled helmet to deflect any man's hope of taming her for marriage. Asked if she had ever met a man who could make her truly happy, she replied, "Sure, lots of times."

Marlene Dietrich brought a sultry Old World decadence to American films in the years before World War II; as an exile from the Weimar Republic, she embodied a restless Germany that would soon become a world menace. Ginger Rogers was the dancing blonde of nonstop legs and resolute smile who helped a generation of weary moviegoers forget their Depression-era deprivations and wartime anxieties. American flyboys languishing in the Pacific Theater adopted Lana Turner and Betty Grable as their favorite Quonset hut pinups. After the war ended, Grace Kelly was the reserved classy beauty who helped women believe they could all become princesses. Under Eisenhower's paternal Cold War reign Marilyn Monroe found success playing steamy, cooing comediennes who triggered seven-year itches in just about every American male. And let us not forget *l'amour* as taught by French phenomena Brigitte Bardot and Catherine Deneuve.

Above: Eva Marie Saint projected a blonde warmth when she appeared in Elia Kazan's On the Waterfront *in 1954. Later, under Alfred Hitchcock's tutelage, she became a cool ice princess.*

Left: Blondes, more often than brunettes, were the victims of tragedies in books and films.

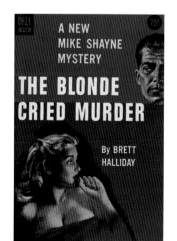

A NEW MIKE SHAYNE MYSTERY

THE BLONDE CRIED MURDER

By BRETT HALLIDAY

Those were the stars, but let's talk about the Blonde Next Door. In 1950 only seven out of a hundred American women dyed their hair. By 1970 the percentage had increased ten-fold, reflecting, perhaps, a Clairol Corporation advertising mantra repeated throughout the 1960s: *If I have but one life to live, let me live it as a blonde.* The message apparently got through, for today more than 40 percent of American women who color their hair choose to be blonde.

The hallmarks of twentieth-century American culture have been invention, social mobility, and the inordinate worship of youth. Notions of blondeness are as wildly protean as

There's no record of what these nightclub bets of 1937 were about, but the blonde seems to be the winner.

they are often silly: The blonde is somehow more of a woman; the blonde is an innocent; the blonde is an indicator of a thoroughbred heritage; the blonde is a wanton woman; the blonde is a trophy of achievement and affluence; the blonde is a bright blossom on the maternal vine, a conduit of genetic allure. The blonde seems to embody every aspect of modern culture.

Blonde women have stirred, inspired, and bedeviled the imaginations of men and women for centuries. This book celebrates the blonde past, present, and future.

This blonde teenager revels in a bed of citrus fruit, circa 1960.

THE FOUNTAIN OF BLONDE YOUTH

According to *Glamour* magazine, natural blondes comprise only 17 percent of American women between the ages of thirteen and sixty-nine. Redheads claim about 4 percent, and ebony tresses 9 percent, while nearly 70 percent are brunettes. But America's doting interest in blondes is only partly a result of limited supply.

"We've been conditioned to consider blondes lovelier," says Dr. Joyce Brothers, who is herself fair-haired. "Even in kindergarten, studies show that eight out of ten boys and girls will paint the little girl's hair blonde. Preferences start early."

Why this preference—part seemingly natural and part cultural myth—for blondes? For one thing, sociologists point out, many people who are blonde in childhood grow up to be something else, forever associating the loss of their flaxen mops with the loss of youth. What, then, is a teenage girl to do when she notices with dismay that the sun no longer reflects warm highlights of youthful gold? A mad dash to the local hairdresser. Sociologist Dr. Thomas Cash of Virginia's Old Dominion College says flatly that "women who convert to blonde do so in the pursuit of youth."

CHAPTER ONE

The Dye Is Cast

*"A chaste woman ought not
to dye her hair yellow."*
—MENANDER, *Fragments*, FOURTH CENTURY B.C.

With rare but persistent exceptions, until this century women lived with the hair color they inherited at birth. Not surprisingly, the ancient Greeks, ever preoccupied with beauty, are credited with the earliest attempts to lighten dark hair. To them, blondness symbolized youth, innocence, superior social standing, and sexual desirability. The god Apollo and the goddess Diana were blonde, while Homer's mythic heroes Achilles, Menelaus, and Paris were depicted as fair-haired. Helen of Troy was said to be a blonde. In *Daring Do's: A History of Extraordinary Hair*, Mary Trasko describes a curious process by which ancient Greek women "lightened their hair by rinsing it in a potassium solution and rubbing it with a pomade of yellow petals and pollen." Men desiring godlike locks dusted their hair with pollen and gold dust.

The fourth century B.C. Athenian playwright Menander recorded a less drastic, more permanent method, one employed by both sexes:

Above: Blondes were the favorite heroines and victims in pulp fiction magazines such as Spicy Mystery, *June 1935.*

Opposite: Detail from Tamara Lempicka's Kizette in Pink, *1926, is a study of blonde youth with a cubist flair. (Collection of the Musées des Beaux-Arts, Nantes. Photo: Giraudon/Art Resource, New York)*

29

Opposite: In the tale of
Sleeping Beauty the
heroine is nearly always
blonde.

Below: Messalina, wife
of the emperor Caligula,
was a nymphomaniacal
brunette who visited the
brothels of Rome wearing
the traditional indicator
of a prostitute at the
time—a blond wig.

"The sun's rays are the best means for lightening the hair, as our men well know. . . . After washing their hair with a special ointment made in Athens, they sit bareheaded in the sun by the hour, waiting for their hair to turn a beautiful golden blond. And it does."

Others used hard soaps and alkaline bleaches that came from Phoenicia (the ancient Greek name for the coastal strip of Palestine-Syria), the soap center of the Mediterranean. If chemicals and sunlight failed to produce acceptable results, the Greeks resorted to wigs, or simply powdered their hair white, gold, silvery white, or red. Cleopatra was just another Mediterranean brunette until she dyed her hair blonde and drove the Romans wild.

Hedonism ran rampant through the upper classes of Roman society under the reigns of emperors Tiberius (A.D. 14–37) and Caligula

(A.D. 41–47). Hair became a conspicuous aspect of noble grooming. Men wore theirs short, while a lady of high social rank typically depended upon domestic slaves for hairdressing services. (A botched dye job on the eve of an important social event could bring fatal consequences to the slave.) Curiously, though blondness was associated with Roman aristocracy, Roman law required prostitutes to wear blond wigs to denote their trade. Emperor Caligula himself wore a blond wig when he embarked on his late-night prowls in search of debauchery.

Rome was a small town with few secrets, not least of all about who was blonde and who was not. The Roman poet Martial (c. A.D. 40–103), who lived and died in Spain, penned a catty bit of poetic gossip about a certain lady who clearly was not:

The lovely hair that Galla wears
Is hers—who could have thought it?
She swears 'tis hers; and true she swears,
For I know where she bought it!

The origin of the word *blonde* traces to the Latin *blondus* ("yellow") and is thought to have immigrated into the English language from France, where by the fifteenth century it had come to mean "yellow-haired." (The French forms persist today: a woman is always *blonde*, while the man is *blond* without an "e.")

From the fall of the Roman Empire in the fifth century A.D. to the fourteenth, there is little evidence that the dyeing of hair was common in Europe, but the fascination with fair-haired women continued to run like a thread through romantic literature. Anonymous Greek verse from the thirteenth century praised a beautiful maiden named Chrysorrhoe: "Her tresses were like rivers, locks full of love; the hair on the maiden's head glowed and flashed brighter than the sun's rays."

33

Opposite: The legendary
Lady Godiva traditionally
has been depicted with long blonde hair. The actual Lady Godiva (c. 1040–80) was the charitable wife of Leofric, the earl of Mercia, who appealed to her husband to lower the taxes on the townspeople of Coventry. He agreed to do this only if she would ride naked through the town. Godiva rode through the town adorned in nothing but her long golden tresses. Leofric kept his word and the taxes were abolished.

Right: Lorelei *by W. Kray. A blonde-haired siren of German legend, Lorelei lured boatmen to shipwreck on the rocky shores of the Rhine River. Heinrich Heine wrote in his poem Die Lorelei: "And yonder sits a maiden/The fairest of the fair,/With gold in her garment glittering,/And she combs her golden hair."*

Virtuous married women of the Renaissance Era were expected to conceal their hair under bonnets or scarves, while single women were allowed to show off their locks as an invitation to courtship. In Italy at least, the display of a well-groomed female mane took on inordinate importance. In his 1548 essay *Of the Beauty of Women*, Agnolo Firenzuola stated in flat terms that "however well-favored a lady may be, if she have not fine hair, her beauty is despoiled of all charm and glory." According to Firenzuola, fine hair meant "fair . . . now of gold, now of honey, and now of the bright and shining rays of the sun: waving, thick, and abundant, and long." (Firenzuola no doubt

Above: In this undated drawing after Sir John Tenniel's nineteenth-century original, Alice holds the magic bottle that will take her to Wonderland. "I must be shutting up like a telescope," she says.

approved of Botticelli's virginal blonde maidens.) To achieve blonde highlights, women sat with their hair draped over the brim of a crownless hat.

By the seventeenth century, the perfumed, powdered, and bewigged ladies of the French court were dictating fashion throughout Europe. Wigs created a brisk export trade in human hair. The convents of the Netherlands were especially sought after for blonde hair, while southern Italian and Turkish women clipped their dark tresses for a little extra money. But to appear as a natural blonde was still preferable, and women were willing to put themselves through considerable unpleasantness to achieve it.

Hairdo historian Mary Trasko records that blonding concoctions often included *ceruse,* a derivative of lead. One recipe called for "a

Left: Spanish noblewoman Lucrezia Borgia (1480–1519) portrayed by Bartolommeo de Venezia. The daughter of Pope Alexander VI, she was the creator of a brilliant Renaissance court in Ferrara (that included the painter Titian). She was not, however, so insulated by royal privilege that she would risk appearing in public on a bad hair day: she postponed one of her three weddings for an entire day so that her long blonde hair could be properly washed, set, and dried.

Marie Antoinette, wife of King Louis XVI, was an ash-blonde fashion-setter who adored high-fashion hair, from wigs to tints. Imprisoned in 1792 on charges of treason for secretly aiding an Austrian counterrevolutionary invasion of France, the thirty-seven-year-old queen's hair turned completely gray. She sent a lock of it to a friend with the inscription "A tress whitened by misfortune." On October 16, 1793, she was beheaded.

quart of lye or a pound of lime . . . mixed with ceruse and warm water, with saffron or turmeric sometimes added to achieve a yellow tone." Trasko continued, "This noxious mix was left on the hair overnight and allowed to dry into a hard shell. The next day it was chipped off, at which point it seems miraculous that any hair should be left on the head!" Catherine the Great of Russia, a natural blonde, didn't have to fiddle with such trying tints.

The high-spirited queen consort of King Louis XVI of France, Marie Antoinette, took European wig fashion to its wildest heights—literally. The Austrian-born royal powdered her hair (a natural ash blonde) and her wigs with wheat starch in hues of blue, pink, violet, and yellow. Some of her dos were three feet high—she once appeared at Versailles with a foot-long replica of a full-rigged French man-of-war sailing on her powdered waves.

After the French Revolution, French fashion and hairstyling turned away from Antoinette-like extremes of artifice and decoration. If wigs were worn, they were lighter, not powdered, and came in a range of colors. In Napoleonic Paris, however, blond wigs remained the overwhelming favorites, so ubiquitous among the capital city's smart set that one author, a social observer named Hennion, was compelled to write and publish *The Secret History of the Blond Wigs of Paris*.

In 1907 a French chemist named Eugene Schueller began manufacturing hair dye in his one-bedroom flat in Paris. During the day he sold the dye, which he called Auréole, to hairdressers of the city. By 1909, he was using the chemical *paraphenylenediamine* as the active ingredient, and had founded the Société Française des Teintures Inoffensives pour Cheveux (French Harmless Hair Dye Company). Two years later Schueller wisely changed the name of his company to L'Oreal, today a market leader worldwide with forty-three thousand employees.

Nearly a century earlier, in 1818, another Gallic chemist by the name of Louis Jacques Thénard had concocted hydrogen peroxide, a chemical now virtually a synonym for the "bottle blonde," but not destined for use in bleaching hair for many years. Peroxide (H_2O_2) has the same ingredients—hydrogen and oxygen—as water (H_2O), but the bleaching agent possesses an extra oxygen molecule, which is liberated as a gas that essentially strips the pigment from the hair fiber.

By the 1920s, double-process blonding was the dominant method. First the hair was stripped of its pigment—leaving it a blank canvas for the hair colorist—and then the desired tone was added. The platinum blonde was achieved with methyl violet or methylene blue. The process, however, was laborious and expensive. In 1931 an American chemist, Lawrence Gelb, returned from a commercial foray in

This beautiful blonde seems to be contemplating the coming Flapper Era.

Left: This 1938 magazine advertisement for L'Oreal Blanc hair dye says, "Platinum Blondes Have It." L'Oreal founder Eugene Schueller began selling hair dye in 1907 in Paris and built it into a global empire.

Opposite: This L'Oreal poster from the 1920s depicted "blonde" hair with a reddish tint.

France with the first oil shampoo tint introduced into America and founded a small company. But the cost of becoming a blonde remained high. Gelb set his chemists to work on a less-expensive formula that would combine the various steps required to change hair color. It took them eight years, but their success firmly established Gelb's fledgling company, Clairol.

With the advent of mass-marketed hair dyes and the encouragement of Hollywood, now almost any woman could become a blonde. By the late 1940s, magazines were instructing women on how to dye their hair at home. In 1950 *Life* magazine assured Americans, in a tone of prissy

If I've only one life . . . let me live it as a blonde!

THE POWER OF ADVERTISING

In 1956 a Manhattan copywriter named Shirley Polykoff (who was a dyed blonde) came up with the famously coy Clairol campaign *Does she or doesn't she? Hair color so natural only her hairdresser knows for sure.* The campaign went on to have a shelf life rivaling that of a canned fruitcake. Clairol's tantalizing riddle "Is it true blondes have more fun?" (also written by Polykoff) brought millions in sales by encouraging women to live their fantasies rather than merely dream them.

In her 1975 book about her adventures in the male-dominated world of advertising, Ms. Polykoff recalled that *Life* magazine executives turned down a ten-page Clairol ad layout because of the double entendre in the phrase

"Does she or doesn't she?" She challenged them to poll the women in their offices. When the dirty-minded executives could not find a single woman who thought the line had anything smutty in it, Ms. Polykoff was not surprised. The ad spread ran on schedule. She later said she knew that any well-brought-up woman of the 1950s—"nice girls" being Clairol's target audience—would never admit to perceiving an off-color meaning—even if they did.

Above: This famous Clairol slogan was written by New York copywriter Shirley Polykoff in the late 1950s.

Left: "Does she . . . or doesn't she?" Another of Polykoff's memorable Clairol slogans.

Does she...or doesn't she?

Hair color so natural only her hairdresser knows for sure!

MISS CLAIROL® HAIR COLOR BATH®

pontification, that "thanks to changed social ideas, it no longer automatically labels a woman 'fast.'" Not surprisingly, later that year *Newsweek* felt that the introduction of a new product called Miss Clairol, which "bleaches, shampoos, and tints simultaneously," merited coverage as a news story. It certainly deserved coverage on the business page. According to a Census Bureau report, in 1939 American dye and tint manufacturers did $1.7 million worth of business; by 1953 it had jumped to $90 million. The credit for this boom was laid to advertising, which tapped into the booming postwar economy with a vengeance, determined to erase public notions of the bottled blonde as an exotic wanton. "Nine out of ten women would choose to be blondes if they could do it by pressing a button," said Clairol chief Lawrence Gelb in 1961. "Nothing ever has induced women to favor dark hair."

Above: Blondes sometimes wintered in Monte Carlo: a 1937 poster by Jean-Gabriel Domergue. (Spencer–Smyth Gallery, San Francisco)

Left: A young woman of the 1930s, fully outfitted to dye and style her hair at home.

CHAPTER TWO

TOP BILLING

"Only God, my dear, | Could love you for
yourself alone | And not your yellow hair."
—WILLIAM BUTLER YEATS,
The Winding Stair and Other Poems (1933)

The silent films of the 1920s were dominated by Gloria Swanson, Pola Negri, Clara Bow, and Louise Brooks—brunettes and redheads—and the auburn Mary Pickford. While the advent of talkies gave a voice to every actor and actress, it especially allowed the new blonde star to project the persona of the Blonde as Wisecracking Vamp. The first of this film breed was a girl from Kansas City, Missouri: Jean Harlow.

Harlow's breakthrough came in 1929 in *Hell's Angels,* an ill-fated talkie about World War I pilots. (The producer was a tall, darkly handsome tycoon by the name of Howard Hughes.) In her role as Helen, she portrayed a one-dimensional vamp who drinks, smokes, and asks men, "Would you be shocked if I put on something more comfortable?"

Critics dismissed the film as mediocre, but her screen presence made eighteen-year-old Harlow an overnight star, as the embodiment of the

Above: Born in 1911 and christened Harlean Carpenter, Jean Harlow was an angelic child with alabaster skin, green eyes, and nearly cotton-white hair. Her mother, a blonde from Kansas City, was a frustrated actress who took Harlean—always known as "The Baby"—to Hollywood. Later she even autographed her daughter's fan mail and photographs.

Opposite: Jean Harlow and William Powell starred in the 1935 MGM romance Reckless.

"New Woman": a sharp-tongued antiheroine who was perfectly comfortable enjoying sex without love, and made no secret of her disdain for naive or priggish men. Her tough and defiant screen persona, however, was pure invention; privately, she deferred to her mother.

Harlow's allure was not lost on Howard Hughes, who wanted a label to promote her. Auburn-haired Mary Pickford was then known as "America's Sweetheart" and redheaded Clara Bow was "The 'It' Girl." After rejecting "Darling Cyclone" and "Contagious Desire" for Harlow, Hughes and his publicity director considered "Blonde Fury," "Blonde Landslide," and then "Blonde Sunshine." Hughes finally settled on "Platinum Blonde," and persuaded Frank Capra, the director of Harlow's new 1931 film, to change its title from *Gallagher* to *Platinum Blonde*.

Hughes launched a huge nationwide publicity blitz. His company organized over three hundred "Platinum Blonde" clubs across the country. A $10,000 prize was offered to any beautician who could chemically match Harlow's hair. No winner was announced, but

Right: Dark-haired film stars like Louise Brooks were overshadowed by Harlow's blazing blonde comet.

Far right: Red-haired Clara Bow was "The 'It' Girl" of silent films in the twenties before Harlow appeared.

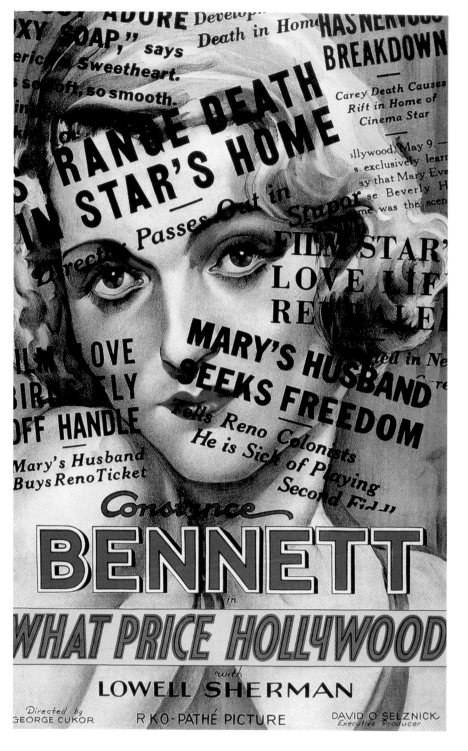

Constance Bennett, a real blonde, appeared in over a dozen silent films, married, and went to Paris, but she returned in 1929 to star in the talkies. Her willowy blonde beauty and husky voice made the RKO-Pathé film What Price Hollywood? a hit in 1932.

TRIALS OF A PLATINUM BLONDE

Jean Harlow was shooting the MGM film *Reckless* in 1935 when her hair—after years of weekly bleaching—became so brittle it broke off her head in lifeless clumps. Marcel Machu, a hair-dye specialist, was brought in to assess the situation. "If they touch her again, she'll have no hair at all," he warned director Victor Fleming.

"It was too late to save her hair," he later recounted. "All I could do was get her through the movie." Sequestering Harlow in a studio bungalow, Machu massaged her head with olive oil for three days until her scalp absorbed it and her hair stopped breaking. Meanwhile, custom-made wigs were ordered from New York to get her through the rest of the picture.

Jean Harlow spent every Sunday at Jim's Beauty Studio on Sunset Boulevard, where a specialist named Pearl Porterfield touched up the star's ash-blonde roots. A decade later Porterfield would do the same for Marilyn Monroe.

peroxide sales skyrocketed and thousands more succeeded in turning themselves into blonde copies of their screen idol.

Although she had appeared as an ash blonde in *Hell's Angels*, Harlow was silver-haired in *Platinum Blonde*. When reporters inquired about her hair-bleaching method, she replied evasively, "I shampoo it every four or five days and put a few drops of liquid bluing in the shampoo soap, not in the rinse water." Years later, one of her hairdressers, Alfred Pagano, revealed the secret of Harlow's silvery tresses: "Peroxide, ammonia, Clorox, and Lux flakes."

Ironically, it wasn't until Harlow donned a wig in the 1932 feature *Red-Headed Woman* that her acting skills and comic timing were noticed. *Red-Headed Woman* was a box-office hit and *Variety* acclaimed her "electric performance."

Left: Clark Gable and Jean Harlow in the last film of her life, Saratoga, 1937. *On black-and-white film, a head of platinum hair could become a glowing halo, an actress a goddess. When the lights shone on Jean, she was luminous.*

Despite her growing success, MGM producer Irving Thalberg felt that it was time for Harlow to change her screen persona. The first thing to be changed, of course, was the color of her hair. The studio's hairdressing department came up with something called "halfway brown," a tint eventually dubbed "brownette."

Harlow liked the new look. "I've always hated my hair," she admitted, "not only because it limited me as an actress, but because it limited me as a person. It made me look hard and spectacular; I had to live up to that platinum quality."

The debut of her new "brownette" look was *Riffraff* (1936), costarring Spencer Tracy, who in a private diary pronounced her "a grand girl." The press thought so, too. "Not even a brunette rinse," opined the *New York Times*, "can dim the platinum potency of her allure."

Her career skyrocketed until May 27, 1937, when Harlow complained of pain in her stomach and left the set of *Saratoga*, a film about

thoroughbred horse racing. Idle gossip credited her condition to poisoning from powerful hair-dyeing chemicals. In fact, Harlow was suffering from a fatal kidney disease, the legacy of a childhood bout with scarlet fever. Ten days later, on June 7, 1937, the twenty-six-year-old died, devastating her lover William Powell and leaving millions of her fans in shock.

Where Jean Harlow had been dominated by her mother and (initially, at least) accepted stardom passively, Mae West largely engineered her own success. As America emerged heroically victorious from World War I and plunged into the Roaring Twenties, there was

Salvador Dalí, Mae West, *1934, gouache with graphite on commercially printed magazine page. (The Art Institute of Chicago. Gift of Mrs. Gilbert Chapman. ©1999 Fundacion Gala-Salvador Dalí/Artists Rights Society, New York)*

something in the air: "Sex o'clock" had struck in America, wrote one journalist. "A wave of sex hysteria and sex discussion seems to have invaded this country." And Mae West was at the forefront.

Born a natural blonde, as West matured her hair turned a lustrous brunette. In 1924, however, she dyed it a golden blonde. Though West had dropped out of grammar school, she had an uncanny ear for tough-guy dialogue of Prohibiton Era speakeasies. She soon became a wisecracking star in vaudeville.

After penning and starring in a string of sexually provocative plays, in 1932 she followed her longtime pal George Raft, a bona fide gangster-turned-actor, to Hollywood. Now thirty-nine, she slimmed off twenty pounds and dyed her hair a Harlow-esque platinum. While the Hays Commission on film censorship solemnly spoke of cinematic threats to the moral fabric of society, Mae went on to make *She Done Him Wrong* for Paramount, a screen version of *Diamond*

Above: The young Mae West was a brunette before dyeing her hair a golden blonde in 1924. This is a rare photo because West didn't like anyone to see her as a nonblonde.

Left: West thumbed her nose at the Flapper Era and wore beaded gowns of the Gay Nineties that suited her busty figure. Born in 1893 in Brooklyn, she sashayed onto her first vaudeville stage at seven, eloped with her song-and-dance partner at eighteen, and took to wearing outlandish gowns and flamboyant hats.

Edward Hopper, New York Movie, *1939, oil on canvas, 32 1/4 by 40 1/8 inches. In this masterpiece, the artist focuses on an isolated blonde usherette lost in her own thoughts. (The Museum of Modern Art, New York. Given anonymously. Photograph © 1998 The Museum of Modern Art, New York.)*

Lil costarring Cary Grant as her love interest. By May 1933 she had broken the box office records set by Greta Garbo and Marlene Dietrich. The following year, West was the fifth most popular star in the country. Her studio salary was the highest of any woman in America. And that made her more powerful than millions and millions of men.

Her career slowed after World War II, and she entered a kind of semiretirement, maintaining her platinum blonde mane and an inspiringly youthful appearance. Even at eighty-seven, she refused to acknowledge having once been anything but a blonde. If a fan asked her to autograph a photograph to the contrary, she'd try to exchange it for another, insisting, "That's not me." And she was right: Mae West—the living trademark she'd become—*had* to be blonde, the way John Wayne was always a cowboy.

Marlene Dietrich's friend Ernest Hemingway affectionately called her "the Kraut." Said he: "If she had nothing more than her voice she could break your heart with it. But she has that beautiful body and the timeless loveliness of her face. It makes no difference how she breaks your heart if she is there to mend it."

When American audiences first saw Josef von Sternberg's 1930 masterpiece *The Blue Angel*, Marlene Dietrich became indelibly associated with the exotic, erotic secrets of the "Old World." Born in 1901 to a strict family in Berlin, the blue-eyed girl with reddish-blonde hair was first known as Maria Magdalena von Losch. Dietrich was seriously considering a career as a violinist when Berlin's theaters and cabarets beckoned. It was a short jump to Hollywood, where her depiction of a tawdry, seductive nightclub singer in *The Blue Angel* made the leggy twenty-nine-year-old an international star.

BLONDE WOMEN

(SUNG BY MARLENE DIETRICH)

You'll try in vain

You can't explain

The charming, alarming blonde women.

They fascinate, they captivate

Beware the amazing blonde women.

Be careful when you meet

The sweet blonde stranger

You may not know it,

But you are reaching danger.

You'll try in vain

You can't explain

The charming, alarming blonde women.

Marlene Dietrich recording in 1952. "All her life she was wearing a mask," said friend Maximilian Schell. "The real Marlene has never been visible. Her mind is filled with the creation of a legend as she conceives it."

"Never before had I met so beautiful a woman," remarked the Austrian-American director Josef von Sternberg. "Nor one who had been so thoroughly discounted and undervalued." Sternberg shared everything he knew about filmmaking with Dietrich, and in return she gave him her best. In *Blonde Venus* (1932), she played a woman compelled to become a prostitute to save her husband. She played a similar part in *Shanghai Express*. She projected a sultry, world-weary magic simply by taking her time in front of the camera.

Before the war, the German authorities tried to lure her back to her native country, but she was an outspoken foe of the Nazis and became an American citizen in 1938. As a dedicated patriot of her new country, she won the affection of millions during World War II by crossing the world to stage front-line USO roadshows and was awarded the Medal of Freedom. She lived to see the reunification of her native Germany in 1990, and died two years later, in Paris, after years of carefully maintained seclusion—determined that the world should remember her as she appears on screen.

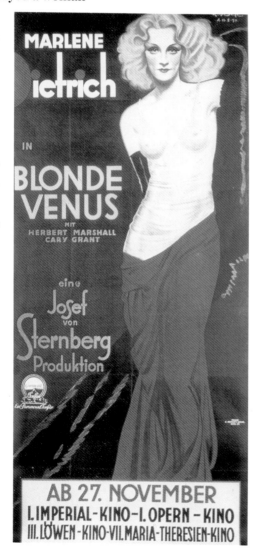

The original poster for Blonde Venus *(Paramount Pictures, 1932) starring Marlene Dietrich. The designer, R. Vogl, made a pointed reference to the statue of the Venus de Milo in masking her arms with black gloves. One was recently auctioned at Sotheby's in 1996 for $25,300.*

Above: Anita Loos wrote Gentlemen Prefer Blondes, *one of the great comic novels of the twenties, originally to amuse her friend H.L. Mencken. It ended up amusing millions in a dozen different languages.*

Opposite: Clare Boothe Luce had just finished her four-year congressional term when she addressed the 1948 Republican National Convention in Philadelphia.

CHAPTER THREE

LITERATURE AND POLITICS

*"Gentlemen always seem
to remember blondes."*

—ANITA LOOS, *Gentlemen Prefer Blondes* (1925)

Gentlemen Prefer Blondes was one of the first modern books to make fun of sex, and it was the first American novel about a specifically blonde adventuress. Written in fractured grammar with florid misspellings, it purported to be the diary of one Lorelei Lee, a footloose, good-hearted gold digger from Little Rock, Arkansas, a flapper with an insatiable appetitite for champage, orchids, and precious stones, who never met a "gentleman" she didn't like.

The brunette author, Anita Loos, was born in the Northern California lumber town of Mount Shasta in 1888, and was writing scripts by the time she was twelve. She broke into Hollywood during the Silent Era, working as an actress and then a screenwriter whose sophistication belied her rural origins. *Gentlemen Prefer Blondes* was her first novel, initially dashed off in 1924 merely as an amusement for her friend H. L. Mencken while he railroaded from New York to Los Angeles. Loos later traced the inspiration for her story to a transcontinental train ride of her own, on which she spied a cute blonde cuddling with a man she recognized as either a Supreme Court justice or a U.S. senator. (Loos recounted the anecdote in different ways to friends over the years.) Mencken, perhaps the most influential American editor and social critic of the first half of the twentieth century, was more than amused; he liked the sketch so much he urged her to expand the "diary entries"—spelling errors and all—into a full-fledged novel.

Loos heeded his advice and wrote the hilarious adventures of a "professional lady" on the make for generous gentlemen in Manhattan, London, and Paris. Lorelei charmed readers with her loopy logic:

Above: Anita Loos and Carol Channing teamed up in 1949 for the Broadway musical version of Gentlemen Prefer Blondes.

Opposite: The original playbill from Gentlemen Prefer Blondes. *(© Al Hirschfeld. Art reproduced by special arrangement with Hirschfeld's exclusive representative, The Margo Feiden Galleries Ltd., New York.)*

So the French veecount is going to call up in the morning but I am not going to see him again. Because French gentlemen are quite deceeving. I mean they take you to quite cute places and they make you feel quite good about yourself and you really seem to have a delightful time but when you get home and come to think it all over, all you got is a fan that only cost 20 francs and a doll that they gave you away for nothing in a restaurant. I mean a girl has to look out in Paris, or she would have such a good time in Paris that she would not get anywheres. So I really think that American gentlemen are the best after all, because kissing your hand may make you feel very very good but a diamond and safire bracelet lasts forever.

The first press run by Boni & Liveright was small—no one expected it to sell—but the book became an instant nationwide hit.

Loos's reputation soon crossed the Atlantic. Edith Wharton, who wrote that "*Gentlemen Prefer Blondes* is the greatest novel since *Manon Lescaut*," insisted on taking Loos to lunch at the Hotel Ritz when she arrived in Paris. Another of Paris's leading literary expatriates, the philosopher, poet, and critic George Santayana, only half in jest called it "the best book on philosophy written by an American." In London, the Prince of Wales complimented her on penning an "entrancing story." Even the Italian dictator Benito Mussolini was a fan. He invited the author to a private audience in Rome where he asked her to autograph his copy of *I signori preferiscone le bionde*. The most impressive praise, however, came from the Irish literary giant James Joyce. "Reclining on a sofa," said the author of *Ulysses*, "I read *Gentlemen Prefer Blondes* for three whole days."

Just what kind of blonde was Lorelei Lee, full of malapropisms but seemingly without malice, who had captured the world's fancy? "Lorelei's gentlemen want to possess her for much the same reason she wants to possess diamonds: she bolsters their egos just as the jewels enhance her self-esteem," wrote Gary Carey in his 1988 biography of Loos. "The jewels are not—as some commentators have suggested—an insurance policy against old age: mentally, Lorelei is too myopic to see beyond the day after tomorrow. . . . She is also perhaps the first courtesan in the history of literature who is not aware of being *declassée*, who genuinely believes herself the equal, if not superior, of any woman who crosses her path." To an America struggling with Yankee egalitarianism and the temptations of social mobility, this was undoubtedly appealing.

Inevitably, however, all this doting on the Blonde Mystique stirred up the majority of women who weren't blonde. Within the resentment lurked envy, but also nascent feminism. Writing in *Good Housekeeping* in 1955, Eleanor Pollock made a biting observation of the

Lorelei Lee's motto was "Kissing your hand may make you feel very good but a diamond bracelet lasts forever." The 1925 edition of Gentlemen Prefer Blondes *was illustrated by Ralph Barton.*

Blonde as Social Tactician: "In my studies of blonde behavior," she noted, "I have seen yellow-haired dynamos who can repair cars, run offices, talk knowingly about the H-bomb, do anything a man can do and do it better. So long as there are no men around. Let one appear, and our golden-haired expert becomes as fragile and helpless as a doe caught in the headlights of an automobile at night. This happens almost overnight, even to the blondes by choice. What's more, it works. I'd like to see any brown-haired damsel get away with it. She'd be treated as if she had rocks in her head. But not our little yellow chickadee."

For every Blonde as Fragile Doe or Yellow Chickadee, there was, according to actress Carol Channing, an ardent herd of Male Enablers. After taking Broadway by storm in 1949 as the first Lorelei Lee in the musical version of *Gentlemen Prefer Blondes*, Channing immediately became the recipient of extraordinary male deference. "Men would take me by the arm and lead me across the street like so many seeing-eye dogs. They sat on the edges of their chairs to hear what I thought about the weather. I didn't have to be bright; I wasn't expected to. All I had to do was be blonde."

*Left: Marie-Therese
Walter was seventeen
when Picasso met her
in Paris in 1932.
She was the muse for
a number of his great
works, including*
The Dream.

This indulgence, she reported later, evaporated just as abruptly after she dyed her hair brunette to appear in another play. "Now," Channing told *Good Housekeeping* in 1955, "I'm just one of the gang. I fight my own way in traffic. I'm interrupted when I open my mouth."

Apparently, however, she preferred the *droits de blondeur,* and adopted the blonde wig that has been her trademark ever since.

Clare Boothe Luce was the antithesis of the dumb blonde. An illegitimate child born into middle-class circumstances in 1903, Clare Boothe married a millionaire at twenty, had a daughter with him, and then divorced him for being a drunk. To be single and divorced in the Jazz Age was either scandalous or provocative, depending upon your point of view. In Clare's circles it was both, so she decided to be a blonde, too. Before long she was the editor of *Vanity Fair* and a celebrated playwright of *The Women,* a venomous comedy about women between marriages or with doubts about matrimony (MGM would film it twice). She married one of the cofounders of *Time* magazine, Henry Luce, and encouraged him to start a picture magazine, which eventually became *Life.*

Clare Boothe Luce had no interest in being just a trophy wife. Following the German invasion of Poland in 1939, she became a war correspondent, reporting from France, and later hopped Pan American "Clippers" to Burma and China to report on Japanese aggressions. In 1942, she successfully ran for a Republican congressional seat in Connecticut. Her ambitions were protean; in a letter to her daughter she asked, "Would it amuse you to have your ma run for Congress and one day get to be a Cabinet minister, or maybe the first lady Vice-President?" She made an unsuccessful run at the U.S. Senate, became a pillar of the Republican party, and was later appointed as America's ambassador to Italy.

By the time she ran for the U.S. Senate from New York in 1964, Clare Boothe Luce had already been a hit playwright, a top journalist, a congresswoman, and an ambassador to Italy. She eventually withdrew from the race—uncharacteristic for a woman Vanity Fair *once described as combining a "fragile blondness with a will of steel."*

The blonde behind the mask is Clare Boothe Luce, American Ambassador to Italy, photographed at a 1954 Press Club Ball in Rome.

In 1951 Evita Peron appeared at this rally to reelect her husband as president of Argentina with her own name on the ticket as vice-president. Evita was credited with giving women in Argentina the right to vote and to legally sue for divorce.

EVITA

Blondes—known as *las rubias*—are rare in Latin American countries. Maria Eva Duarte—later known as "Evita"—was born into dire poverty in the small town of Los Toldos, Argentina. At night, watching movies projected outdoors onto a mottled plaster wall or a bedsheet, she was captivated by the images and dreamed of becoming an actress.

She arrived in Buenos Aires in 1935 at fifteen and pursued her dream with a hard-nosed pragmatism, getting parts in radio soap operas and meeting a young army colonel, Juan Domingo Peron, who became her lover. As Peron's political fortunes rose, Evita wanted to discard the social stigma of her past as a *morocha*—the unsympathetic Argentine expression for a dark-haired, lower-class woman. It became an obsession. The first step was to transform herself into a blonde.

"It was a theatrical and symbolic gold," says biographer Alicia Dujovne Ortiz, "a gold that

Evita Peron rose from poverty to control Argentinean politics with her husband, General Juan Peron. In this photo she was visiting Paris in 1947. On seeing her entourage enter Notre Dame, Cardinal Roncalli (the future Pope John XXIII) exclaimed: "The Empress Eugenie has returned!" Her ambition increased after this European voyage, and she announced, "What I want is to pass into history."

imitated the effect of the golden halos and backgrounds of the religious paintings of the Middle Ages. This art isolated holy bodies, distanced them from the earth, from heaviness and from density." The transformation to vivid blondness and theatricality entranced the imaginations of the devoutly religious *descamisados*, the desperate "shirtless poor" of Argentina, whose hope would be renewed by Evita's promises of social reform and assistance.

In October 1945, Juan Peron's political foes succeeded in arranging his arrest on trumped-up charges of treason. Famous in spite of her status as Peron's unwed consort, Evita took to the airwaves and beseeched the masses to rally in support of her imprisoned lover. The streets filled, panicking Peron's enemies, who quickly released him. Peron, now a general, married her out of gratitude. A year later, he became president of Argentina.

Eva Peron toured the country championing the rights of women, laborers, and the poor. In the summer of 1951, she declared her candidacy for vice-president of the country. Alarmed by her fervent support among the politically restive *descamisados*, the Argentine military sent a

Above: Eva Peron addressed workers in 1952. She acquired a multimillion-dollar collection of furs and jewelry, insisting that "The poor like to see me lovely, they don't want to be championed by some lady who doesn't dress well. They dream of me and I cannot disappoint them."

Left: A two-peso stamp honored Evita.

warning, and Eva backed out of the race. She died at thirty-three in the summer of 1952. The official radio bulletin announcing her death began with the words "Our spiritual leader is gone!" She was buried in an immaculate white dress and went on to become a mythic—and controversial—figure for millions of Argentinians.

An unapologetically ambitious woman, Luce lived during an age when the nation was still trying to figure out how women were supposed to behave. Novelist and historian Gore Vidal wrote that "after Eleanor Roosevelt, Clare was easily the most hated woman of her time—she was too beautiful, too successful, in the theater, in politics, in marriage." Is it possible that if she hadn't dyed her hair, she wouldn't have gone as far as she did? Given the number of journalistic references, both admiring and hostile, to her bottled blondeness, one wonders. Regardless, in the public eye she was not merely Clare Boothe Luce—but also "That Blonde."

Anthropologist Jane Van Lawick-Goodall with a curious chimpanzee at the Gombe Stream Research Center in Nigeria in 1972. In the 1970s, Dr. Goodall spent nine months a year studying chimps along the shores of Lake Tanganyika and the other three months teaching Stanford students.

THERE ARE BLONDES AND BLONDES

BY RAYMOND CHANDLER, FROM *THE LONG GOODBYE*, 1953

There are blondes and blondes and it is almost a joke word nowadays. All blondes have their points, except perhaps the metallic ones who are as blond as a Zulu under the bleach and as to disposition as soft as a sidewalk. There is the small cute blonde who cheeps and twitters, and the big statuesque blonde who straight-arms you with an ice-blue glare. There is the blonde who gives you the up-from-under look and smells lovely and shimmers and hangs on your arm and is always very very tired when you take her home. She makes that helpless gesture and has that goddamned headache and you would like to slug her except that you are glad you found out about the headache before you invested too much time and money and hope in her. Because the headache will always be there, a weapon that never wears out and is as deadly as the bravo's rapier or Lucrezia's poison vial.

There is the soft and willing and alcoholic blonde who doesn't care what she wears as long as it is mink or where she goes as long as it is the Starlight Roof and there is plenty of dry champagne. There is the small perky blonde who is a little pal and wants to pay her own way and is full of sunshine and common sense and knows judo from the ground up and can toss a truck driver over her shoulder without missing more than one sentence out of the editorial in the *Saturday Review*. There is the pale, pale blonde with anemia of some non-fatal but incurable type. She is very languid and very shadowy and she speaks softly out of nowhere and you can't lay a finger on her because in the first place you don't want to and in the second place she is reading *The Waste Land* or Dante in the original, or Kafka or Kierkegaard or studying Provençal. She adores music and when the New York Philharmonic is playing Hindemith she can tell you which one of the six bass viols came in a quarter of a beat too late. I hear Toscanini can also. That makes two of them.

And lastly there is the gorgeous show piece who will outlast three kingpin racketeers and then marry a couple of millionaires at a million a head and end up with a pale rose villa at Cap d'Antibes, an Alfa-Romeo town car complete with pilot and copilot, and a stable of shopworn aristocrats, all of whom she will treat with the affectionate absent-mindedness of an elderly duke saying goodnight to his butler.

Opposite: French wildlife filmmakers Monsieur and Madame Armande Denis peering from the elephant grass in Uganda and looking for the right shot, 1952.

Ernest Hemingway had a lifelong fascination with blondes. His third wife, Martha Gellhorn, was a blonde—a natural one—tall and beautiful; they met in 1936 at Sloppy Joe's bar in Key West. It was the beginning of a four-year affair and a short-lived marriage.

They had many adventures together, from China to Paris. In 1940 they bought a house in Cuba, but Gellhorn was soon off to Europe as a war correspondent. Hemingway followed, but his wife's determination to live as independently as he did led to bitter clashes. As the war ended, so did their marriage. Following the liberation of Paris, Hemingway was writing love poems to Mary Welsh, a *Time* magazine correspondent stationed there.

Mary Welsh was also fair-haired, in her words a "peanut butter blonde." Hemingway called her his "pocket Rubens." But after their marriage, Hemingway wanted her blonder. In her autobiography, *The Way It Was*, she recounts her transformation: "I submitted to the bleaching and Ernest was entranced by the results. Deeply rooted in his field of aesthetics was some mystical devotion to blondness, the blonder the lovelier, I never learned why. He would have been ecstatic in a world of women dandelions."

Hemingway himself once lightened his hair, telling someone who asked about it that he had "accidentally" used some of his wife's hair lightener. It was about this time—still angry over his tumultuous relationship with Martha Gellhorn, now sentimentally in love with Mary Welsh—that he began writing his ambivalent portrait of Catherine Bourne in *Garden of Eden*, a woman who bleaches her hair white-blonde—and then convinces her husband to do the same. Perhaps it should have been called *The Sun Also Bleaches*.

Above: Mary Hemingway, the author's fourth wife, dyed her hair even blonder to please Papa.

Opposite: Ernest Hemingway and his third wife, journalist Martha Gellhorn, with a brace of Idaho pheasants. Her intelligence and independence attracted and later infuriated the author.

CHAPTER FOUR

THE GOLDEN BLONDE

*"Blondes are considered interesting merely if
they are agreeable. If a blonde is funny, she is
considered to have a spectacular personality."*
—HAROLD BRODKEY, *Men's Life*, 1990

*Above: Doris Day—born
Doris von Kappelhoff in
Cincinnati in 1924—was
the quintessential Sunny
Blonde of the postwar era.
She became an instant star
in 1948 in the pleasantly
silly* Romance on the
High Seas.

*Opposite: A sunny blonde
on the cover of the* Saturday Evening Post, *June
15, 1935.*

Emerging from the Depression Era,
an increasing number of dyed blondes gave America a new look of
youth and vigor. Somewhere between the Park Avenue heiresses and
the Hollywood starlets were millions of women thought of as The
Blonde Next Door—the can-do gals who were now euphemistically
"treating" rather than "dyeing" their hair blonde. Commercial advertising seemed to feature blondes because they caught the eye, not
only of men but of other women. Blondes were the yellow daisies in
a somewhat drab urban world created by dark-haired men in gray
flannel suits.

The forties were booming years for blondes in Hollywood. In
1946–47, newspapers reported that Betty Grable was the highest-
paid woman in America, earning $300,000. Her studio, Twentieth
Century Fox, had insured her legs for $1 million—more, it was noted,

than the policies on the appendages of Marlene Dietrich and Fred Astaire. "Everyone has a gimmick," Grable allowed late in her life, "and I've been standing on mine for years." Her roles were predictable: usually a sunny, somewhat naive small-town girl trying to make it in showbiz.

During World War II, Grable was the most popular pinup girl. Thousands of GIs tacked her image to the walls in their barracks, and carried it into battle wrapped in cellophane. Her appeal, wrote biographer Patrick Agan, was pure Blonde as Girl Next Door. "Betty was witty and wisecracking, warm and quite wonderful, stretching what she herself always thought was a minor talent into a bouncy legend." There was nothing exotic or aloof about her—nothing to make a GI

Right: These blondes helped the boys at the front.

Far right: A young "Rosie the Riveter" working on the home front during World War II.

Opposite: Betty Grable.

Lovely things happen to you in a

Catalina

	These enhance a small bosom		
Snug Harbor $14.95		Gingerbread Man $12.95	Bandolier $17.95
Continental $25.00	Dots and Dashes $15.95	These slim the upper leg	Peg O' My Heart $19.95
These flatter a long torso	Sun Sticks $10.95	Encore $19.95	Water Witch $15.95

It's hats off to the charms of a girl who wears a Catalina swimsuit!

Catalina styles are not only high fashion, they show off your particular figure. That's because of Catalina's priceless way of making swimsuits flatter different figure types.

The Catalina Glamour Guide above shows which swimsuits will do most for you. Why not take this chart with you when you shop?

For name of nearest store, write: Catalina, Inc., 443 S. San Pedro St., Los Angeles 13, California.

Shown: First Mate. Batiste Lastex with white middy trim. $12.95.

© *Catalina, Inc., a division of Julius* **KAYSER** *& Company hosiery · lingerie · gloves*

Tan with TARTAN

For him... and him... and him...

"I pledge myself to guard every bit
of Beauty that he cherishes in me"

*Left: Here the blonde hair
and blue eyes speak pa-
triotically of loyalty and
devotion in wartime ro-
mance.*

*Opposite: This blonde
seems to have her eye on
the admiral's cap.*

think she wouldn't be waiting for him when he got back. "She epito-
mized the kind of girl that any guy, with a little luck, might meet"—if
they could just survive the war. She was, in her own words, "the kind
of girl that truck drivers love." In 1944 the Eighth Air Force, a celebrated wing of the Army Air Corps, christened a B-17 bomber the
"Betty Grable." The fuselage of another Superfortress was adorned with
a full-color pinup painting of her.

Grable exuded a reassuring wholesomeness, distinct from the sultry swagger of Mae West and from the sophisticated, international
allure of Marlene Dietrich. Her private life didn't disappoint: she
married the bandleader Harry James, settled in on the couple's ranch,
and doted on their two daughters.

She was content to enjoy her time in the sun, and she was
gracious when she costarred with the up-and-coming Marilyn

Monroe in *How to Marry a Millionaire* (1953), not complaining when Monroe was given top billing. The story goes that when she saw that Marilyn was about to eclipse her as the Blonde du Jour, she said, "Honey, I've had mine. Go get yours." She only made one more movie after that. Monroe took over her dressing room at Twentieth Century Fox.

In the forties the cinematic spotlight swung away from the platinum blonde to the golden blonde. Veronica Lake, billed as the Peek-a-Boo Blonde, starred opposite William Holden in *I Wanted Wings* in 1941. Audiences were enthralled by her languid, unruly spun-gold hair that had a habit of falling over her face, concealing one alluring eye. (After Pearl Harbor, the War Department asked Paramount to

Left: Veronica Lake was a Paramount star when she appeared in this 1947 magazine advertisement. In all she appeared in over twenty films, including Hold That Blonde *(Paramount Pictures, 1945), before dropping out of Hollywood.*

Happy Resolution for a Happy New Year!

Cadillac

Left: The status of this Eisenhower-era Cinderella was echoed by the golden highlights of her hair and the blonde Cadillac.

Opposite: The blonde cheerleader always gets her man, or vice versa. This game took place in Seattle, Washington, in 1955.

change Lake's trademark bangs—so many women working in defense plants, adopting the style, were getting their hair caught in machines that the peek-a-boo posed a serious hazard.)

Postwar Hollywood saw in Doris Day the female incarnation of every returning GI's dream girl. Curiously, though, in roughly three of every four films in which Day starred, she played an urban career woman, not a housewife. She was the "working gal" that a harried but self-assured businessman of the fifties was supposed to overlook at first, then notice, get to know, get to like, and inevitably fall in love with. Typically, Day's character would be married by the film's end, becoming at last a perky paradigm of domesticity.

While American moviegoers basked in the folksy small-town charm of Betty Grable and Doris Day, a new type of blonde also glided onto the stage, the Ice Princess. She was the fair-haired aristocracy, as elegant as she was—or seemed to be—inaccessible.

The Ice Princess seemed most natural in urban settings, driving in a Cadillac convertible, standing atop a windblown skyscraper, or boarding a jet to Paris. She occupied the best table at El Morocco, trailing admiring male glances wherever she went, always at the center of every high-society ball. She was all refinement and good bone structure, and she was blissfully exempt from messy, complicated personal relationships, let alone a job—unless she was the boss or

Above: Don't try this at home—at least not without a structural engineer on hand. In 1954, Lucia Danzinger, wife of an Austrian hairdresser, entered the World Championship Hairdressing Competition at Brighton, England.

Opposite: Grace Kelly's performance in The Country Girl *(1954) earned her the New York Drama Critics' Circle Award and an Oscar.*

Blonde gossip flies on the set of the TV show American Bandstand, *1958.*

LIFE

NEW RADIANCE FOR AMERICAN CHURCHES

THE MODERN RENAISSANCE OF STAINED-GLASS ART

A GARDEN OF SHRUBS TO PLANT NOW

GRACE KELLY,
WINNER OF THE
ACADEMY AWARD

20 CENTS

APRIL 11, 1955

REG. U. S. PAT. OFF.

Above: The two leads, Grace Kelly and Cary Grant, pose for a publicity shot for Hitchcock's To Catch a Thief *(Paramount Pictures, 1955). According to Grace's biographer Robert Lacey, Hitchcock once had Grace kiss her leading man's forehead thirty times, just so he could watch.*

the boss' daughter. She seemed to value men mainly as fashion accessories—that is, until love or disaster broke down her frozen ramparts to reveal volcanic passions within.

The quintessential Hollywood prototype of the Ice Princess was Philadelphia-born Grace Kelly, who famously abandoned film stardom in 1956 to become Princess Grace of Monaco. She had a restrained sex appeal, and audiences sensed something simultaneously traditional and modern about her. It gave her a distinctive credibility, and is perhaps why she made sixty television commercials between 1950–53. Her big breaks came in the Western classic *High Noon*, in which she starred opposite Gary Cooper, and in *Mogambo* with Clark Gable.

Her cinematic career clicked up a notch when she captured the attention of Alfred Hitchcock, who saw in Kelly the embodiment of his notion of the perfect "woman of mystery." The *auteur* confessed to a recurring fantasy—of being in a taxi with a beautiful but chilly blonde, in his words a "Snow Princess," whose inhibitions suddenly melt in a passionate fire. "The English woman or the North German or the Swedish can look like a schoolmarm, but boy," he said, "when they get going, these women are quite astonishing. . . . It is more interesting to discover the sex in a woman than to have it thrown at you!"

The blonde's natural habitat, of course, is Scandinavia, Northern Europe, and the Slavic countries. A silvery Finn or a golden Swede walking down the swarthy streets of Naples or São Paulo turns heads and draws wolf whistles, but few would blink an eye in Helsinki or

Stockholm. The blonde's power to excite is greatest where she is in a minority. "Now you take a blonde in Hollywood and what do you find? Another dandelion in a field," wrote detective novelist Mickey Spillane. "But put a blonde out in Japan and down in sultry South America where raven tresses are the norm, and something happens. The dandelion stands alone, gleaming. Brilliant sunshine at midnight."

Above: The blonde gets a stamp of approval.

Left: Prince Rainier and his princess in New York in 1956. Upon hearing of Kelly's engagement, fellow star Marilyn Monroe told her, "I'm so glad you've found a way out of this business."

HITCHCOCK'S BLONDE OBSESSION

Alfred Hitchcock was unapologetically obsessed with blondes, and he cast them in nearly every one of his films—think of Janet Leigh in *Psycho*, Kim Novak in *Vertigo*, and Tippi Hedren in *Marnie* and *The Birds*. Significantly, his women are often murder victims. "Blondes are the best victims," he explained. "They're like virgin snow which shows up the bloody footprints."

Hitchcock saw Grace Kelly's controlled blonde magic and showcased her in *Dial M for Murder*, *Rear Window*, and *To Catch a Thief*.

Above right: Janet Leigh first lightened her brownish hair in 1949. That made her perfect to star in Hitchcock's shriek-making Psycho *(Paramount Pictures, 1960).*

Right: In the climax of Hitchcock's thriller Vertigo *(Paramount Pictures, 1958), Jimmy Stewart pushes Kim Novak out of the bell tower.*

Opposite: Hitchcock and his discovery, Tippi Hedren, while shooting The Birds *(Universal Pictures, 1963).*

Top: As spy Eve Kendall, Eva Marie Saint offers advertising-man-turned-fugitive Cary Grant refuge in her train compartment in Hitchcock's North by Northwest *(MGM, 1959).*

Bottom: Eva Marie Saint and Cary Grant escape evil agents by climbing down Lincoln's nose at Mount Rushmore.

The director was entranced by her beauty, but he never made a pass at Kelly; instead, like the voyeur in *Rear Window,* he put it all on film.

Eva Marie Saint was another serious actress who put a twist on the blonde as Ice Queen. In Hitchcock's eerie 1959 thriller *North by Northwest,* she plays a cool, highly efficient spy, apparently in the service of a malevolent foreign country. Cary Grant, intrigued by Saint's suave mystique, becomes ensnared in a web of political doublecrosses. At first Saint, as Eve Kendall, seems intent on destroying the hapless Grant, but out of love she saves him and reveals her true mission as a spy for the American government. By the end, they have destroyed the forces of evil together, and Saint's once-tough facade has given way to passion. Hitchcock ends the film with a happy movie-image cliché—as Grant and Saint embrace eagerly, the train they are on hurtles into a dark tunnel.

*In the final scene, Cary Grant and Eva Marie Saint
embrace just as their train hurtles through a tunnel.*

CHAPTER FIVE

VA-VA-VOOM

"O Marilyn, bombshell of bombshells, blond
of our dreams, tease, promise, and embodiment
of desire, where are you now?"
—VICKI GOLDBERG, *American Photo*, MAY/JUNE 1997

The fifties were a potent time for sexuality in America. In 1948, while Doris Day remained ascendant as the celluloid embodiment of the Golden Blonde that every clean-cut American desired, the Kinsey Report shocked the nation with statistical analyses revealing the sexual habits of its citizens. In 1953 Hugh Hefner launched the first issue of *Playboy*, publishing nude photos of a very young Marilyn Monroe.

The American economy soared ever higher, and the tailfins on cars swelled, along with women's busts and bouffant hairdos. The time was ripe for the Blonde as Bombshell, a new, over-the-top, *va-va-voom* icon. She arrived in the form of Jayne Mansfield.

Born Vera Jayne Palmer in Bryn Mawr, Pennsylvania, in 1933, Mansfield was the daughter of a successful attorney who died of a heart attack when she was three. By age seventeen Jayne had a

Above: Steaks and fried chicken were the specialties at Fitz's Drive-in of West Palm Beach, Florida, in the 1960s, but it was cheesecake on the matchbook.

Opposite: Detail from Andy Warhol's Marilyn, *1962. Acrylic on canvas, 70 by 80 inches. Warhol had just finished showing his Campbell's Soup series in Los Angeles in August 1962 when he learned of her death. Within days he began the Marilyn series. Here he reproduces the movie star's face so often it becomes a crowd of masks, leaving her individual personality far behind. (Tate Gallery, London. Art Resource, New York)*

forty-inch bust, a B average in high school, and a burning ambition, kindled by movie magazines, to be an actress. Her role model was Shirley Temple. Yearning to start her climb to fame, Jayne left the University of Texas, her husband, and her daughter to take a Hollywood screen test for the role of Joan of Arc. She didn't get the part.

She did, however, acquire a publicity agent, who cannily suggested she dye her dark hair platinum and change her name. But serious acting didn't follow. At Christmas in 1954 her PR man dressed her up as a skimpily clad Santa Claus and had her deliver bottles of whiskey to reporters at the Los Angeles newspapers. The journalists were

Right: Sophia Loren displayed serious concern over Jayne Mansfield's overflowing bustline in the late fifties.

Opposite: Jayne Mansfield's approach to the world might best be summed up in the words of her husband, Mickey: "She is deeply religious in many ways but is one of the best twisters in the country. She does not consider it undignified or forbidden."

pleased. In 1955, she got a small role in the Jane Russell film *Under-water!*, and at the Florida premiere she startled reporters by appearing (uninvited) at the site of Russell's scheduled photo session in a minuscule bikini whose top "accidentally" burst open and fell into the hotel pool. The photographers snapped pictures in a frenzy.

Jayne appeared in *Playboy* in 1956 and landed a film contract with Warner Brothers. Her basic career plan was to go over the top whenever possible, and America loved it. She walked ocelots along Hollywood Boulevard and dyed her poodles to match her gowns. She barreled around Los Angeles in a vivid pink Jaguar, a color that would become her trademark. That same year she found true love with Mickey Hargitay, a former Mr. Universe with a fifty-one-inch chest who was working as a chorus dancer in Mae West's revue. They

"JAYNE! JAYNE! BEND OVER! BEND OVER!"

Screenwriter Mark Hugh Miller never forgot a chance encounter in 1961 he had with Jayne Mansfield and her husband, Mickey Hargitay, in San Francisco, aboard the Hawaii-bound luxury liner Matsonia:

"The Matson steamship company used to have open houses, so you could mingle with passengers aboard ship in the hours before sailing. We got there just as Mansfield and Hargitay were making a photo appearance on the fantail. I'd never seen anything like it—the *paparazzi* thing, a real movie star. But Jayne—my God! Tanned like coffee with cream, with pale lipstick, this huge gleaming head of platinum hair—and a scoop-neck tight white dress with spaghetti straps and white high heels. And Hargitay looking like a blond Atlas in a gray suit and white shirt unbuttoned halfway to his belt, standing back with his hands in his pockets, grinning broadly as his wife struck poses for the cameras.

"The photographers were shouting 'Jayne! Jayne! Bend over! Bend over!' She put her knee on a chaise lounge, leaned forward and flashed this wall-to-wall smile. She pulled her shoulders

Jayne Mansfield's approach to acting was to go over the top, or to lose the top entirely. Miami writer Ted Austin described her well in a recent Ocean Drive *magazine: "All tits and dizziness, a peroxide reverie who was strong, sure and willing to do anything for a publicity opportunity, she became a symbolic ambassador of the good life and about as subtle as a 1956 Cadillac."*

back to accentuate her bust. I was weak at the knees. The photographers kept shouting for more, and she obliged. What strikes me today—when that kind of silliness would be considered sexist—is how good-natured and innocent it seemed. It was a moment in a different time. It was like watching Sinatra rehearse a song or sneak a smoke. It was a wonderfully goofy performance that I was lucky to see."

BARBIE WAS A BLONDE

One of the greatest modern-day blonde personalities is a tiny eleven-and-one-half-inch-tall plastic doll called Barbie. She was created in 1959 by Elliot and Ruth Handler, owners of Mattel, who named her after Barbie, their doll-crazy thirteen-year-old daughter. (Ken was named after their son.) By 1964, the company sold $5 million worth of dolls per year—plus 25 million pieces of clothing—resulting in a $97 million-a-year industry. Barbie herself received fifteen thousand fan letters per week in 1969. Three decades later, Barbie is still a billion-dollar bonanza for the Mattel company, which sells one doll every two seconds. What distinguished Barbie from all previous dolls for children was that she was not modeled after a helpless child that needed nurturing. She was a young adult, presumably of voting age, with a sense of style (clothes) and adventure (employment, travel, romance) and a diaphanous nightdress to entice Ken. Although Barbie comes with various hair colors, the iconic color has always been blonde.

Over one billion Barbies have been sold since the doll first appeared in 1959.

married and bought a Beverly Hills mansion with a heart-shaped pool in which, Jayne coyly confided, she did the breaststroke.

In 1957 Mansfield signed a contract with Fox for $1,250 a week and costarred with Tony Randall in 452 performances of the Broadway hit *Will Success Spoil Rock Hunter?*, a spoof on Marilyn Monroe's career.

She made a film *Kiss Them for Me* with Cary Grant, but she never got the serious parts. Mansfield's career waned as the fifties drew to a close, forcing her take to the road, appearing in nightclubs, local dinner theaters, and state fairs. Late one night in June 1967, after playing a club in Biloxi, Mississippi, Jayne and her lawyer, Sam Brody,

A blonde receiving the attention of dark-haired men on Italy's Adriatic Coast, 1961.

Right: Swiss actress Ursula Andress and Peter O'Toole in Woody Allen's sex farce What's New Pussycat? *(United Artists, 1965). Andress's name, appropriately, sounds like "undress" when spoken with her pan-European purr. In* Pussycat, *Andress parachutes into O'Toole's convertible as he heads for a "naughty weekend" at Chateau Chantelle, a French version of the No-Tell Motel.*

Opposite: In a gown that left no room for lunch, Diana Dors (born Diana Fluck in 1931) was England's blonde response to Marilyn Monroe and Jayne Mansfield.

embarked in a new Buick to New Orleans. Jayne's three children were asleep in the back seat. Around 2 A.M., Brody slammed into the rear of a slow-moving mosquito abatement sprayer truck. Jayne, who had once been crowned "Miss Freeway," died instantly, as did Brody. (Her children escaped injury.) Photographs of her platinum blonde wig lying on the pavement spawned a persistent myth that she was decapitated, which is untrue.

To photographer Cecil Beaton, Marilyn Monroe was as "spectacular as the silvery shower of a Vesuvius fountain, an incredible display of inspired, narcissistic moods." She had a special relationship with the camera lens. "God gave her everything," said director Billy Wilder. "The first day a photographer took a picture of her she was a genius."

Monroe's odyssey is a fascinating and tragic tale that has inspired more than six hundred books. As Norma Jean Baker she had her first screen test at Twentieth Century Fox in 1946, but her career was slow in taking off until she dyed her brown hair platinum blonde. It was no coincidence that the bleach and dye specialist she hired to do it was Pearl Porterfield, the Sunset Boulevard colorist who had served Jean Harlow. Monroe had been enthralled with Harlow since childhood. "I used to look at movie magazines and cut out the pictures of Jean Harlow," she recalled. "That's what I wanted to be one day—a Jean Harlow."

Above: A natural brunette, the young Monroe turned blonde only when a job for a shampoo ad hinged on it. She found her new hair unsettling. "I couldn't get used to myself," she told a friend.

Her first two showcase roles were *The Asphalt Jungle* and *All About Eve* (both 1950), which encouraged Fox to cast her in *Gentlemen Prefer Blondes* with Jane Russell in 1953. Nine years later, she told a reporter for *Life*: "I remember when I got the part in *Gentlemen Prefer Blondes*, Jane Russell—she was the brunette in it and I was the blonde—she got $200,000 for it and I got my $500 a week, but that to me was, you know, considerable. . . . The only thing was I couldn't get a dressing

Brigitte Bardot played Camille in Jean-Luc Godard's masterpiece, Contempt *(Les Films Concordia/Rome Paris Films, 1963). A retelling of Homer's* Odyssey, *the film celebrated Bardot's voluptuousness and intelligence.*

BRIGITTE BARDOT: FRENCH SEX KITTEN

The French have always had a fascination for blondes. Brigitte Bardot was twenty-four when, in 1957, director Roger Vadim's *And God Created Woman* made her an international star and "sex kitten." A legend was carefully crafted around her seemingly childlike, occasionally disturbing character. Vadim, who became her first husband, presented her not as an actress but as "a phenomenon of nature," a kind of living totem. "She doesn't act," he explained. "She exists."

Even the Left Bank existentialist-feminist philosopher Simone de Beauvoir pondered Bardot's undeniable originality, pronouncing her "the most perfect specimen of ambiguous nymphs. Seen from behind her slender, muscular, dancer's body is almost androgynous. Femininity triumphs in her delightful bosom. The long voluptuous tresses of Melisande flow down to her shoulders, but her hairdo is that of a negligent waif. The lines of her lips form a childish pout, and at the same time those lips are very kissable. . . . It has often been said that her face has only one expression. It is true that the outer world is hardly reflected in it at all and that it does not reveal great inner disturbance. But that air of indifference becomes her."

room. . . . I said, 'Look, after all, I am the blonde and it is *Gentlemen Prefer Blondes*.' Because still they always kept saying, 'Remember, you're not a star.' I said, 'Well, whatever I am, I *am* the blonde.'"

Monroe yearned to be more than a comic blonde icon; she wanted to be respected as a serious actress. Determined to bring it about, she abruptly left Hollywood to study Method acting at Manhattan's famed Actors Studio with the autocratic Lee Strasberg. The studio's recent alumni included Marlon Brando, Paul Newman, Joanne Woodward, and Montgomery Clift. To master the Method, Monroe took to reading Freud, Tolstoy, and Dostoyevsky. Through the same sheer force of will that transformed her from a bobby-soxer into America's sex queen, she acquired the skills of a trained thespian. Fox offered her more money and lured her back to the West Coast. She gave audiences an indelible performance in *Bus Stop* (1956), and her studies with Strasberg left her with a lifelong hunger for meatier roles.

She enchanted the nation when she married revered New York baseball star Joe DiMaggio in 1954. Then she surprised the nation by divorcing Joe and marrying the cerebral Pulitzer Prize–winning playwright Arthur Miller, author of *The Death of a Salesman*. As had happened with DiMaggio, Monroe and Miller simultaneously loved and bewildered each other. Drugs—particularly prescription tranquilizers and sleeping pills—made a discreet and fateful entry into her life. Her mercurial personality began to take wider mood

Marilyn upstaged Jane Russell in Gentlemen Prefer Blondes *and in this* Life *magazine cover, 1953.*

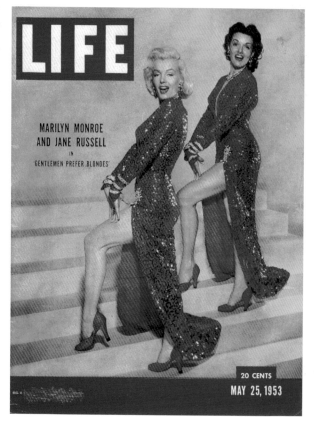

swings, producing temper tantrums and ever-ready tears, which nearly drove Billy Wilder nuts when he directed her in his 1959 comedy classic *Some Like It Hot*. (For one of its scenes, in which Tony Curtis eats a chicken leg, Wilder had to shoot forty-two takes before Marilyn got her lines right. The experience put Curtis off Monroe—and chicken—for some years.) She acquired the reputation of being "difficult."

Though still married to Miller, Monroe started a much-publicized affair with the debonair French leading man Yves Montand during the shooting of the appropriately titled *Let's Make Love* (1960). Miller took the high road of silent dignity, and eventually they reconciled. In 1961, they journeyed together to a Nevada location near Reno for the shooting of the John Huston film *The Misfits*, written by Miller and costarring Clark Gable and Montgomery Clift. Monroe's performance was captivating, and though critics panned Miller's heavy-handed tale of cowboys on a brutal hunt for wild horses, it was the

Right: Splendor in the grass, 1954. Mae West said, "The only gal who came near me in the sex-appeal department was pretty little Marilyn Monroe. All the others had were big boobs."

Opposite: Monroe with husband Arthur Miller, leaving a New York hospital after her miscarriage in 1957.

closest Monroe would come to realizing her dream of mastering a serious role. It also proved to be her last film (as well as Gable's).

The title of Monroe's next movie, *Something's Got to Give*, echoed the feelings of those who were close to her. Her discipline on location was poor. In the middle of the shoot, she flew to New York City to sing her notoriously vampy version of "Happy Birthday" to President John F. Kennedy in front of twenty thousand guests at Madison Square Garden. Monroe and Kennedy had spent the weekend together a few weeks earlier in California, at Bing Crosby's Palm Springs hideaway. Kennedy roared with laughter at Marilyn's passionate singing, remarking in his speech afterward that he had never heard the birthday song sung in such a "wholesome" manner.

By this time, the square, soft-spoken DiMaggio had come back into her life, and they were making plans to remarry—but it was not to be. In the early hours of August 5, 1962, police found Monroe in

Tom Wesselmann, Great American Nude, #57, *1964. Synthetic polymer on composition board, 48 by 65 inches. (Collection of Whitney Museum of American Art, New York. Photo: Sandak, Inc./Macmillan & Co., New York/ © Tom Wesselmann/ Licensed by VAGA, New York)*

Willem de Kooning,
Marilyn Monroe, *1954.*
Oil on canvas, 50 by 30
inches. (Collection of the
Neuberger Museum of
Art, Purchase College,
State University of New
York. Gift of Roy R.
Neuberger. Photo: Jim
Frank)

"How Marilyn Monroe Dyed Her Hair"

BY SIMONE SIGNORET, FROM *NOSTALGIA ISN'T WHAT IT USED TO BE*, 1978

Every Saturday morning the hair colorist of the late Jean Harlow would board her plane in San Diego and arrive in Los Angeles, where Marilyn's car would be waiting for her at the airport and would bring her to our kitchen, or rather the kitchenette of Bungalow No. 21.

Before allowing her to remove the bottles from her old carrying bag (products long since made obsolete by more modern techniques), Marilyn would ply her with food from a buffet—a combination of brunch and cocktail party ingredients—she had carefully prepared. The old lady would indulge with gusto. Marilyn would knock on my door, telling me to bring my towels, and then the hair-dyeing party would begin.

Now the old lady began to relive her life. While the two of us blonded, she would tell all about the color she had concocted for Jean Harlow's head thirty years earlier, which had been the secret of her success. Her tales were full of silk dresses, white foxes, lamé shoes, and parties. They were full of silences—for she preferred not to tell everything she might have

told. Her stories always ended with the funeral of the "platinum-blond bombshell." While she talked, the two of us wallowed in nostalgia, winking at each other when the old lady would stop in her tale because she was too full of emotion to go on. Then her stick with the cotton swab at the end, coated with the precious liquid that was supposed to be applied to the

Marilyn as Lorelei Lee in Gentlemen Prefer Blondes *(Twentieth Century Fox, 1953)*.

daily, conjugal, and amorous life of her star, nor of course from her deathbed.

After another meal, she would take her plane back to San Diego. When she left the two of us would be impeccably blond— Marilyn platinum and I on the auburn side. Then Marilyn and I would clean up the kitchen, since the artist had always left a lot of cotton swabs lying around on the floor.

It amused me enormously to have my hair tinted by the lady who pretended to have created the myth who was splashed across the newspaper pages of my adolescence. But it didn't amuse my neighbor. It was no accident that she had tracked down the address of this retired lady. She believed in her. She liked her and respected her. She was perfectly willing to pay for her round trips from the Mexican border, her limousine rides, and her caviar. It was a kind of association though a third person between the Blonde Mark I and the Blonde she turned into. And in retrospect I think it was also a hand stretched out to someone who had been forgotten.

equally precious roots of our hair, would fly through the air instead of coming down, lending an incalculable factor to the incubation time of this delicate operation. As Marilyn worried only about her widow's peak, there, things became serious; when it was a question of the enemy, the stick must not fly through the air. But the rest of the time she would sink back and let herself be rocked in the cradle of the old lady's anecdotes.

As soon as the widow's peak had been treated in seriousness and silence, the old lady, punctuating her story with "dearies," "sweeties," and "sugars," would take up her tale where she had left off. Listening to her, you might come to the conclusion that Jean Harlow had her hair dyed twenty-four hours out of the day, since it would appear that this lady had never been absent for a minute of the

her bed, a casualty of either suicide or an accidental overdose of barbiturates and Nembutal. Conspiracy theorists spun fantastic scenarios of government and Kennedy family involvement in her death (and still do). The truth is far simpler: Monroe's comet burned out because of her emotional fragility.

Her demise, at age thirty-six, was front-page news. Millions wondered who the woman was who had fascinated so many people for so long. Among them was novelist Norman Mailer, who published his biography *Marilyn* eleven years after her death. "So we think of Marilyn," he mused, "who was every man's love affair with America, Marilyn Monroe who was blonde and beautiful and had a sweet little rinky-dink of a voice and all the cleanliness of all the clean American backyards."

Another of her many biographers, Donald Spoto, explained her broad appeal. "Although in herself she transcended America's fantasies by constant effort at self-perfection," he wrote, "Marilyn simultaneously represented those fantasies. She was the postwar ideal of the American girl, soft, transparently needy, worshipful of men, naïve, offering sex without demands."

Billy Wilder concurred: "She was never vulgar in a role that could have become vulgar, and somehow you felt good when you saw her on the screen. To put it briefly, she had a quality no one else ever had on the screen except Garbo. No one."

Late in her life, Monroe posed as Harlow in a *Life* magazine feature photographed by Richard Avedon. She also expressed interest in starring in *The Jean Harlow Story*. After reading a maudlin treatment for the film, however, she rejected the idea, saying, "I hope they don't do that to me after I'm gone."

Below: A quiet moment on location during the filming of The Misfits *(United Artists, 1961). The film would be her last.*

It wasn't a coincidence that Edward Hopper painted a Marilyn-like blonde in 1962, the year Marilyn died. Hopper had always been fascinated with the cinema. Edward Hopper, New York Office, 1962. Oil on canvas, 40 by 55 inches. (Collection of the Montgomery Museum of Fine Arts, Montgomery, Alabama, The Blount Collection)

*Above: Supermodel
Cheryl Tiegs in the original Black Velvet ads of
the 1970s.*

*Opposite: Drew
Barrymore in New York
City.*

EPILOGUE

GALLERY OF POSTMODERN BLONDES

*"I'm not blonde to be more fun; I'm blonde
because it looks better."*

—CYBILL SHEPHERD, *Glamour*, 1990

It is impossible to look at a blonde to-
day without thinking of stars of the past—Mae West, Marlene
Dietrich, Grace Kelly, and Marilyn Monroe. Madonna and Kim
Basinger fill the scorecard for some, but do they match the swagger
of Diamond Lil, the sultry top-hatted singer in *The Blue Angel,* or
Kelly's elegant sex appeal in just about every film she ever made?
The world changed when Norma Jean's dream died on that Los An-
geles night in 1962, and so did the Blonde.

While the icon, and the society that created and worshipped it, has
never been the same since that moment, the blonde mystique has never
completely faded. It's less strong, perhaps, less all-encompassing, but

117

it is as ubiquitous as ever, maybe more so as women have taken more prominent positions in all aspects of society. In Hollywood during the sixties and seventies, we were mesmerized by Faye Dunaway as she robbed banks with Warren Beatty in *Bonnie and Clyde,* dined orgiastically with Steve McQueen in *The Thomas Crown Affair,* and nursed Jack Nicholson's switchblade-sliced schnozzle in *Chinatown.* Jane Fonda, despite so many superb screen performances, will never be forgotten as also having played the space-age blonde bimbette *Barbarella.*

Right: Twiggy, the mod fashion model of swing-ing London, in 1967.

Opposite: Julie Christie in David Lean's epic film Dr. Zhivago *(MGM, 1965).*

Right: Cybill Shepherd was a fashion model before Peter Bogdanovich cast her in The Last Picture Show *(Columbia Pictures, 1971).*

Opposite: Goldie Hawn (born Goldie Jean Studlendgehawn in 1945) shrewdly morphed herself from sixties ditz into a respected Hollywood producer and megastar.

Above: Jane Fonda in Barbarella *(Paramount Pictures, 1968).*

Music and fashion continued to glorify blondes. The seventies rocked to Blondie, the punkish persona of Debbie Harry, who has also been reincarnated as a brunette. In "Harry's House-Centerpiece," the blonde sage Joni Mitchell warned us of "beauty parlor blondes with credit card eyes" looking for "the chic and the fancy to buy." The poignant echo left by Marilyn Monroe's soft voice was mixed into Madonna's calculated blonde trajectory of the 1980s. "Being blond is definitely a different state of mind," said Madonna in *Rolling Stone.* "I can't really put my finger on it, but the artifice of being blond has some incredible sort of sexual connotation."

If Marilyn struggled to be taken seriously as a blonde actress, today a glamorous cadre of respected actresses—Sharon Stone, Michelle Pfeiffer, Jessica Lange, Meryl Streep, Meg Ryan, and Jodie Foster, among others—hold the blonde banner high, along with a good many Oscars.

Madonna performing à la Marilyn at the 1991 Academy Awards.

BLONDES: A CELEBRATION

BY PETER GERSTENZANG, *COSMOPOLITAN*, MARCH 1991

And the men, you ask? Many have told me, oh-so-wistfully, that they are still searching for their fantasy lady and that she is blonde. Although some still seek the classic beach bunny, others invoke the artsy blonde, the classic beatnik. She writes poetry or paints. Her childhood was troubled. She is misunderstood. Sometimes she acts tough and streetwise, which is when he knows she needs the most protection. Or maybe she's a songwriter who whispers plaints of alienation from behind a Steinway in a café where no one is listening. Except him. A beret figures in her wardrobe, and she wears a couple of earrings in one ear.

But enough of angst and artistic endeavor. Let me celebrate another sort of blonde entirely, one who, if she never actually went away, is back bigger than ever. She's the happily trashy blonde, usually dyed, who makes no apology for her fake hair or glittery frocks. Yes, I'm talking about the bimbo, the blonde bombshell—a compliment, by the way. She's the kind who pops from cakes, steals men from their wives, even sings rock 'n' roll. Face it, these are trashy times, and as a result, such girls are cleaning up.

Left: Cameron Diaz.

Middle: Gwyneth Paltrow.

Right: Meg Ryan.

The fashion industry keeps searching for the quintessential postmodern blonde icon, presenting and promoting supermodels like the boyish Twiggy in the sixties, the all-American Cheryl Tiegs in the seventies, the twinkling Christie Brinkley in the eighties, and the satiny Claudia Schiffer in the final decade of the millennium. The fashion mavens who introduce them to us have an unapologetic bias in favor of the flaxen-haired. "How many truly unforgettable brunettes can you remember?" asks Eileen Ford, president of the Ford modeling agency in Manhattan. "Blondes have greater longevity." In 1995 designer Gianni Versace unveiled a white-flower perfume called Blonde, its fragrance purportedly enabling women to live a "blonde moment" without changing their hair color.

In 1981, twenty-year-old brown-haired Diana Spencer caught the eye of England's Prince Charles. For their wedding she became a blonde, and during their marriage she became blonder. In

"I'd like to have myself declared legally blonde."

Right: Jodie Foster.

Middle right: Sharon Stone.

Far right: Michelle Pfeiffer and Jessica Lange.

1997 the storybook celebrity who had found purpose in motherhood and in helping the unfortunate died in a tragic car crash, stunning the global village. "You were a Cinderella at the Ball and now you are a Sleeping Beauty," an anonymous fan wrote on a funeral remembrance. Perhaps she best represented the modern blonde icon in all her serious/sexy complexity.

Today, blondes are everywhere, not symbolizing any one idea but reflecting all aspects of society, from angry blonde punks with nose rings and the bikini-strung *Baywatch* "babes" to the wannabe Ivana Trumps of Manhattan and the Diane Sawyer news anchor clones on the networks. There is also an impressive battalion of blondes taking the national political stage, and who could ignore one of the most influential blondes of our media age—Martha Stewart—she who knows how to make everything Just So?

Of course beauty—and a good many of the traits and proclivities ascribed to blondes—originates in the eye of the beholder. All women are beautiful in their own way, whether blonde, brunette, or redhead. I must admit, however, that I'm fascinated with blondes and the concept of blondness. And that great philosophical conundrum still remains: Is it true, after all, that blondes *do* have more fun?

Diana, Princess of Wales.

Mel Ramos, Chiquita, 1964. Oil on canvas.
70 by 60 inches. (Private Collection, New
York. © 1996 Mel Ramos/VAGA)

BIBLIOGRAPHY

Agan, Patrick. *The Decline and Fall of the Love Goddesses*. Los Angeles: Pinnacle Books, 1979.

Amis, Martin. "The Mirror of Ourselves." *Time,* September 15, 1997, p. 64.

Ashton, Dore. *Picasso On Art: A Selection of Views*. New York: The Viking Press, 1972.

——"Barbie Doll Set." *The Nation*, April 27, 1964, p. 407.

Bess, D. "Menace of the Barbie Dolls." *Ramparts*, January 25, 1969, pp. 26–27.

Burgess, Anthony. *But Do Blondes Prefer Gentlemen?* New York: McGraw-Hill, 1986.

Carcopino, Jérome. *Daily Life in Ancient Rome*. New Haven: Yale University Press, 1968.

Carey, Gary. *Anita Loos*. New York: Alfred A. Knopf, 1988.

Chandler, Raymond. *Farewell, My Lovely*. New York: Vintage Crime/Black Lizard, 1992.

——*The Long Goodbye*. New York: Vintage Crime/Black Lizard, 1988.

Corson, Richard. *Fashions in Hair: The First Five Thousand Years*. London: Peter Owen Ltd., 1965.

"Diana Princess of Wales." *People* tribute, Fall 1997.

Eames, John Douglas. *The MGM Story*. New York: Crown Publishers, 1979.

Ellrod, J.G. *The Stars of Hollywood Remembered*. Jefferson, North Carolina: McFarland & Company, 1997.

Evans, David. *Glamour Blondes: From Mae to Madonna*. London: Britannia Press Publishing, 1995.

Frank, S. "Brunette Today, Blonde Tomorrow." *Saturday Evening Post*, September 9, 1961, pp. 20–21, 45.

Gerstenzang, Peter. "Blondes . . . A Celebration!" *Cosmopolitan*, March 1991, pp. 192–195.

Harbinson, W.A. *Evita: Saint or Sinner?* New York: St. Martin's Press, 1996.

Hemingway, Mary Welsh. *How It Was*. New York: Alfred A. Knopf, 1976.

Hotchner, A.E. *Hemingway and His World*. London: Viking, 1989.

"Jayne Mansfield." *Ocean Drive*, October 1997, p. 163.

Kay, Karyn, and Gerald Peary. *Women and the Cinema: A Critical Anthology*. New York: E.P. Dutton, 1977.

Krauze, Enrique. "The Blonde Leading the Blind." *New Republic*, February 10, 1997, p. 31.

Lacey, Robert. *Grace*. New York: G.P. Putnam's Sons, 1994.

Lawrenson, Helen. "Blondes Get all the Breaks." *Esquire*, January 1941, pp. 28–29.

Leider, Emily Wortis. *Becoming Mae West*. New York: Farrar Straus Giroux, 1997.

Loos, Anita. *Gentlemen Prefer Blondes*. New York: Boni & Liveright, 1925.

Mailer, Norman. *Marilyn*. New York: Grosset & Dunlap, 1973.

March, Joseph Moncure. *The Wild Party*. New York: Pantheon Books, 1994.

McCracken, Grant. *Big Hair*. Woodstock, New York: The Overlook Press, 1996.

McDonough, Yona Zeldis. "What Barbie Really Taught Me." *New York Times Magazine*, January 25, 1998, p. 70.

Morris, Desmond. "The Anthropology of Blondes." *Men's Life*, Fall 1990, pp. 104–110.

Morris, Sylvia Jukes. *Rage for Fame: The Ascent of Clare Boothe Luce*. New York: Random House, 1997.

Panati, Charles. *Panati's Extraordinary Origins of Everyday Things*. New York: Perennial Library, 1987.

Pollock, Eleanor. "Blondes Lead Wonderful Lives." *Good Housekeeping*, February 1955, pp. 64–65.

Schultz, Patricia. "All-American Blondes." *Harper's Bazaar*. February 1991, pp. 154–157.

Shulman, Irving. *Harlow: An Intimate Biography*. San Francisco: Mercury House, 1964.

Signoret, Simone. *Nostalgia Isn't What It Used to Be*. New York: Harper & Row, 1978.

Spoto, Donald. *The Art of Alfred Hitchcock*. New York: Anchor Books, 1992.

——*Blue Angel: The Life of Marlene Dietrich*. New York: Doubleday, 1992.

——*The Dark Side of Genius: The Life of Alfred Hitchcock*. New York: Ballantine, 1983.

——*Marilyn Monroe: The Biography*. New York: Harper Collins, 1993.

Steinem, Gloria. *Marilyn*. New York: MJF Books, 1986.

Stenn, David. *Bombshell*. New York: Doubleday, 1993.

"This Lady is Dyeing Her Hair." *LIFE*, November 22, 1955, pp. 113, 115–116.

Thomson, David. *A Biographical Dictionary of Film*. New York: Alfred A. Knopf, 1996.

Trasko, Mary. *Daring Do's*. Paris: Flammarion, 1994.

Vadim, Roger. *Bardot, Deneuve, Fonda: My Life with the Three Most Beautiful Women in the World*. New York: Simon and Schuster, 1986.

"Veronica Lake's Hair." *Life*, November 24, 1941, pp. 58–61.

Vidal, Gore. "The Woman Behind The Women." *New Yorker*, May 26, 1997, pp. 70–76.

Zinzer, William K. "Barbie Doll: Million $ Business." *Saturday Evening Post*, December 12, 1964, pp. 72–73.

PICTURE CREDITS

Catherine Deneuve electrified filmgoers as a bored bourgeois housewife in Luis Buñuel's Belle de Jour *(Allied Artists/Alta Films, S.A., 1967). In the film, Deneuve's character escapes a dull life by working at a brothel while her spouse is at his office.*

INDEX

Page numbers in bold indicate
photographs.

A

Andress, Ursula, **102**
Astaire, Fred, **22,** 78

B

Barbie, 100
Bardot, Brigitte, 25, **106**
Barrymore, Drew, **116**
Belle de Jour, **128**
Bennett, Constance, **47**
Birth of Venus (Botticelli), **37**
Blondie, 120
Borgia, Lucrezia, **36**
Botticelli, Sandro, 36, **37**
Bow, Clara, 45, **46**
Brinkley, Christie, 123
Brooks, Louise, 45, **46**
Brothers, Dr. Joyce, 27

C

Caligula, 30, 33
Catherine the Great, 38
Chandler, Raymond, 13, 72
Channing, Carol, **60,** 64, 66
Christie, Julie, **119**
Cinderella, **32**
Clairol, 25, 41, **42,** 43
Cleopatra, 30

D

Dalí, Salvador, **52**
Danzinger, Lucia, **86**
Day, Doris, **77,** 85–86, 95, **130**
de Beauvoir, Simone, 106

de Gelman, Natasha Z., **63**
de Kooning, Willem, **111**
Deneuve, Catherine, 25, **128**
Denis, Armande, **73**
de Venezia, Bartolommeo, **36**
Diana, Princess, 123–124, **125**
Diaz, Cameron, **123**
Dietrich, Marlene, **19,** 25, **55,**
    55–57, **56, 57,** 78
DiMaggio, Joe, 107, 110
Domergue, Jean-Gabriel, **43**
Dors, Diana, **103**
Dream, The (Picasso), **65**
Dunaway, Faye, 118

E

Ekberg, Anita, **104**

F

Firenzuola, Agnolo, 34
Fitzgerald, F. Scott, 14
Fonda, Jane, 118, **120**
Ford, Eileen, 123
Foster, Jodie, 120, **124**
Frightened Girl (Lichtenstein),
    10

G

Gable, Clark, **22, 49,** 88, 108,
    110
Garbo, Greta, 55
Gelb, Lawrence, 39, 41, 43
Gellhorn, Martha, **74,** 75
Gentlemen Prefer Blondes, 59–
    64, 105, 107, **112**
Gerstenzang, Peter, 122
Gibson, Wynne, **4**

Goodall, Jane Van Lawick-, **71**
Grable, Betty, 25, 77–82, **79**
Grant, Cary, 55, **88, 92, 93,** 101
Great American Nude
    (Wesselmann), **110**
Great Gatsby, The (Fitzgerald),
    14

H

Halliwell, Leslie, 16, 18
Handler, Elliot and Ruth, 100
Hargitay, Mickey, 98, 99
Harlow, Jean, **12,** 13, 16, **44,**
    45, 45–51, **48,** 105, 114
Harry, Debbie, 120
Hawn, Goldie, **121**
Hayworth, Rita, **24**
Hedren, Tippi, 90, **91**
Hefner, Hugh, 95
Helen of Troy, 29
Hell's Angels, 45, 49
Hemingway, Ernest, 55, **74,** 75
Hemingway, Mary, **75**
Hitchcock, Alfred, 22, 25, 88,
    90–93, **91**
Hopper, Edward, **54, 115**
Hughes, Howard, 45, 46
Hydrogen peroxide, 39

J

Joyce, James, 62

K

Kelly, Grace, 25, **87, 88, 89,** 90
Kennedy, John F., 110
Kizette in Pink (Lempicka), **28**
Kray, W., **34**

L

Lady Godiva, 34, **35**
Lake, Veronica, **82**, 82–85, **83**
Lange, Jessica, 120, **124**
Leigh, Janet, **90**
Lempicka, Tamara, **28**
Lichtenstein, Roy, **10**
Lombard, Carole, **22**
Loos, Anita, **59**, 59–60, **60**, 62
L'Oreal, 39, **40, 41**
Lorelei (Kray), **34**
Loren, Sophia, **96**
Luce, Clare Boothe, **58, 66, 67,** 71

M

Machu, Marcel, 48
Madonna, 120, **122**
Mailer, Norman, 114
Mansfield, Jayne, 95–101, **96, 97, 99,** 105
March, Joseph Moncure, 16
Marie Antoinette, **38**
Menander, 29, 30
Mencken, H. L., 59, 60
Meseke, Marilyn, **21**
Messalina, **30**
Miller, Arthur, 107, 108, **109**
Miller, Mark Hugh, 99
Misfits, The, 108, **114**
Mitchell, Joni, 120
Monroe, Marilyn, **11**, 14, 25, 48, 81–82, 89, **94**, 95, **105,** 105–114, **107, 108, 109, 111, 112, 114,** 120, **132**
Mussolini, Benito, 62

N

Negri, Pola, 45
New York Movie (Hopper), **54**
New York Office (Hopper), **115**
North by Northwest, **92, 93**
Novak, Kim, **23, 90**

P

Paltrow, Gwyneth, **123**
Peron, Evita, **68, 69,** 69–70, **70**
Pfeiffer, Michelle, 120, **124**
Picasso, Pablo, **65**
Pickford, Mary, 45
Platinum Blonde, 46, 49
Playboy, 95, **98**
Pollock, Eleanor, 20, 62–63
Polykoff, Shirley, 42
Porterfield, Pearl, 48, 105
Powell, William, **44,** 51

R

Ramos, Mel, 126
Rivera, Diego, **63**
Rogers, Ginger, **22,** 25
Russell, Jane, 98, 105, **107**
Ryan, Meg, 120, **123**

S

Saint, Eva Marie, **25, 92, 93**
Santayana, George, 62
Schiffer, Claudia, 123
Schueller, Eugene, 38, 41
Shepherd, Cybill, 117, **120**
Signoret, Simone, 112, **113**
Sleeping Beauty, **31**
Some Like It Hot, 108

Spillane, Mickey, 89
Spoto, Donald, 114
Sten, Anna, **50**
Stewart, Martha, 124
Stone, Sharon, 120, **124**
Strasberg, Lee, 107
Streep, Meryl, 120
Swanson, Gloria, 45

T

Thénard, Louis Jacques, 39
Tiegs, Cheryl, **117,** 123
Trasko, Mary, 29, 36–38
Turner, Lana, **8–9,** 25
Twiggy, **118,** 123

V

Vadim, Roger, 106
Versace, Gianni, 123
Vidal, Gore, 71
Vogl, R., 57
von Sternberg, Josef, 55, 57

W

Walter, Marie-Therese, **64**
Warhol, Andy, **94**
Welsh, Mary, 75
Wesselmann, Tom, **110**
West, Mae, **18,** 25, **51,** 51–55, **52, 53,** 108
Wharton, Edith, 62
What's New Pussycat?, **102**
Wilder, Billy, 105, 108, 114
Will Success Spoil Rock Hunter?, 101

Opposite: Doris Day helped create a new cinematic sub-genre, the innocent romantic comedy—a notion well-suited to audiences of the strait-laced fifties. Day pushed her hands into wet cement in front of Grauman's Chinese Theater on January 19, 1961.

Following page: Good-bye Norma Jean, 1956.

Does she...or doesn't she?

If I've only one life . . . let me live it as a blonde.